# PRAISE FOR
# PUSHING BACK ENTROPY

"*Pushing Back Entropy* is one of the most powerful, insightful, and impactful 'team bible' books I have read. It is filled with critical practical integration processes and methodologies for building healthy teams and preventing conflict for intrapersonal and interpersonal growth and fulfillment in both personal and organizational environments. I believe author Andy Johnson's dream and passion for a world with less conflict, where people learn to value each other, and a world of healthy relationships of trust and vulnerability will emerge by applying the valuable teachings, wisdom, and knowledge presented in this masterpiece for living a healthy life and building healthy teams and organizations. This is a must-read-and-apply book for all aspiring healthy individuals and team builders—probably the best book you will read this year!!"

**— Imelda Butler, Chairperson at Odyssey Transformational Strategies and Odyssey Consulting Institute**

"Based on the powerful universal principle of entropy, this book is, without a doubt, a novel and refreshing examination of an old topic on the 'dynamics' of teams. It is a must read for those interested in teams and team building, as it presents a thought provoking yet credible paradigm for team building in the twenty-first century."

**— Dr. Shayne Tracy, Strategic Organization Development Specialist, Trusted Advisor, and Master Executive Coach**

"Andy Johnson's book, *Pushing Back Entropy*, looks at the causes and conditions of both team decay and team health. Andy first details the causes of conflict and how to deal with it. Next, he explores the pieces and parts that make up a healthy team. Taken together, these two parts of the book can help any team that is serious about performance improvement. If you have anything to do with creating and maintaining effective teams, buy this book."

**— Randy Lisk, Executive Coach and Founder of Lisk Associates**

"Communication, especially the conversations we have with each other, forms the heart and soul of a high-performing team. In *Pushing Back Entropy*, Andy Johnson wisely places communication as the skill that encircles team members holding these vital relationships together. He will show you how. You'll want to keep this book on your desk and refer to it often."

**— Shawn Kent Hayashi, Executive Coach and author of *Conversations for Change, Conversations for Creating Star Performers*, and *Conversations That Get Results and Inspire Collaboration***

"There are certain laws that govern our universe. One of them is the law of entropy, the second law of thermodynamics; things move from order to disorder. Gardens need weeding. Ornamental trees need trimming. A new house soon needs paint and maintenance. And teams move from order to disorder, from functionality to dysfunction. *Pushing*

*Back Entropy* is a must-read book that brilliantly charts a path forward to eliminate team dysfunction and replace it with robust team health."

**— Melvin D. Nelson, President and CEO of Executive Management Systems, Inc.**

"Andy's *Pushing Back Entropy* is filled with information, knowledge, and wisdom gained from his broad and deep background and experience in understanding human nature and behavior. This is an excellent read and resource for improving individual and team effectiveness. More than a quick read, *Pushing Back Entropy* has found a prominent place in my bookcase."

**— Dr. Carol Gaffney, President and CEO of Starr Advantage Group**

"It's rare to find a business book that's so well informed and thoughtful. *Pushing Back Entropy* examines what it takes to build healthy teams from a wide range of perspectives including behavioral styles, emotional intelligence, ethics, and more. It's a gem of a resource. I know I'll refer to again and again, for myself and my clients."

**— Dr. Nancy Buffington, Executive Communications Coach and Owner of Boise Speakwell**

In *Pushing Back Entropy* Andy Johnson proposes an insightful and original model of the mechanisms that cause and contribute to conflict. More importantly, he proposes practical solutions for building teams that are resistant to conflict-related decay. This is essentially a book about affecting results by creating team health. Andy's experience as a business person, therapist, and coach allows him a unique and interesting perspective. Readers, whether managers, leaders, parents, or consultants, will better understand and be equipped to counteract the seemingly ever-present effects of conflict.

**— Gordon Holland, Director Leadership Development, Western States Equipment Company**

"Andy provides a robust framework with actionable objectives for leaders committed to the continued focus and intentional strategy required to push back entropy and build an exceptional team."

**— Andrew Brady, Coach and Director of Business Development at The XLR8 Team, Inc.**

PUSHING BACK

# entropy

MOVING TEAMS FROM
## CONFLICT
## TO HEALTH

ANDY JOHNSON

**Pushing Back Entropy:** Moving Teams from Conflict to Health
By Andy Johnson

For further information about speaking engagements, professional consultation, special bulk pricing, or other related inquiries, see the author's websites at www.introvertrevolution.com and www.price-associates.com.

Cover Design: Cari Campbell, Cari Campbell Design
Interior Design: Fusion Creative Works, www.fusioncw.com
Primary Editor: Kim Foster

Print ISBN: 978-0-9893390-1-8

Library of Congress Control Number: 2013920508


First Printing
Printed in the United States of America

Published by Restoration Publishing

# DEDICATION

This book is dedicated to my dear wife, Sherri, the better half of our marital and parenting team. Two are better than one. I've learned, slowly but surely, to fully embrace the results that will only come from shared leadership. You are an integral part of everything I do and am. I couldn't do any of it without you. I love you. Thanks for being my partner in this adventure called life. Hopefully, together, we're pushing back entropy and moving our family system toward health for the sake of the girls and future generations.

# ACKNOWLEDGMENTS

This book is comprised of two separate and yet highly interconnected topics. The study of conflict has been a personal focus
for much of my professional life. I was circumstantially drawn
into studying conflict. It is more of an assignment by fate than
by choice. The directly related topic of team building has been
an area where I have been greatly influenced through the instruction of one of my key mentors, Ron Price. Several years
ago, Ron began to teach me his model of "The Disciplines of
Extraordinary Teams." The second half of this volume is highly
influenced and shaped by Ron's work in this area. I will footnote
where I can clearly show the connection. I am aware, however,
that my entire model is highly influenced at more points than
I can reference by my relationship with Ron. So, Ron and I will
be a model of teamwork. In a healthy team, it is often hard to
determine the original source of contributions. The team works
with such synergy that the results truly are shared. Thanks, Ron,
for sharing in my personal journey.

Target Training International (TTI) was founded in the 1980s
by Bill Bonsttetter. Ron introduced me to TTI several years ago.

Since that time, Bill and the team have been both a direct and indirect shaping influence in my coaching philosophy. The three appendices (behavioral styles, core motivators, and emotional intelligence) are descriptive of these three topics as measured in assessments for each generated by TTI. Ron Ernst, another TTI associate, has contributed to my understanding through his seminar, book, and related materials called *RealTime Coaching*.

I learned a lot about functioning as a team in the context of the core leadership team at Johnson Architects. Scott Freeman and Walt Lindgren taught me much about the nature of healthy teams. The years we worked together as a leadership team continue to inform my model. Those were some of my most satisfying and rewarding years, and it was due in largest part to the great working environment we cocreated. We experienced many of the intrinsic rewards I describe in chapter 12. Thanks, Scott, for reading the manuscript and offering such helpful critiques and suggestions.

My first job out of college was working for Wolff Lang Christopher Architects Inc. in Rancho Cucamonga. There I had the privilege of working with Larry Wolff. We were organized into design teams, and I was fortunate to be placed on team Wolff. Larry taught me many valuable principles, which are reflected in this book. Chief among them was the key place of integrity and respect for others. Larry modeled the character traits I describe in the team section of this book.

My deepest thanks once again to Maryanna Young and the team at Aloha Publishing. Cari Campbell has once more come up with a great cover that communicates the message of this book. Thanks to Kim Foster for all her hard work in editing this to make it all it can be. Shiloh Schroeder at Fusion Creative Works has done a great job with the interiors and graphics. I couldn't have done this without all of you. You guys make me look good.

# CONTENTS

# FOREWORD

"Good to great!" If I have heard this phrase once, I have heard it a thousand times. When Jim Collins published his book *Good to Great: Why Some Companies Make the Leap . . . and Others Don't*, that phrase immediately resonated with leaders around the globe. No matter where I am privileged to serve, leaders regularly tell me, "We want to take our team from good to great!" They often tell me that their organization is already successful, and rightfully so. But they aren't satisfied. They want to take their leadership team and the organization to the next level of performance, culture, and vitality.

But what does it really take to go from good to great? Jim Collins established his definition of greatness using extrinsic measures, based on stock returns over a fifteen-year period. His "great" companies outperformed the "good" companies by an average of seven times. His researchers took a detailed look at these companies and developed a formula for moving to the elite level. Their results revealed new insights into leadership, hiring practices, focus, and contribution. (Ironically, several of Jim Collins' examples of great organizations have fallen from grace since his book was published in 2001.)

In this book, Andy Johnson takes a more intrinsic look at moving from good to great. What kinds of relationships and collaboration does it take for a team to be truly extraordinary?

When asked by our clients about moving from good to great, I immediately wonder about the difference between wants and commitments. Would any leader confess, "I don't really want to go from good to great"? None that I have met in my forty-five-year career. And yet, it is the rare leader who demonstrates the commitment of focus, resources, and discipline that persuades me this is a serious pursuit, for which they have counted the cost and committed their future reputation.

So, what does it take to build a truly great team? Nobody defines this better than Andy in *Pushing Back Entropy: Moving Teams from Conflict to Health*. Great teams, or as I often describe them, extraordinary teams, are extraordinary in part because they are so uncommon. Extraordinary team performance comes from at least three aspects of preparation:

1. Extraordinary hiring, onboarding, and development. Really great teams are rarely comprised of superstars. Instead, they are made up of ordinary people who do extraordinary things because their talents are aligned beautifully and intelligently with their assignments and they have a healthy sort of "chip on their shoulders," an inner drive to prove something that results in extraordinary motivation.

2. Extraordinary teams practice being a team, and they use their team building to know one another and connect at deep levels, both relationally and purposefully. This commitment to relational bonding and deep clarity of purpose creates a hidden strength that folks like

Jim Collins respect but cannot measure. (After all, as W. Edwards Deming taught us, not everything of value can be measured.) As Andy points out with exceptional expertise, a big part of this relational and purposeful bonding comes from learning together how to move from conflict to health.

3. Extraordinary teams know their mission with such clarity and intensity that they are blind to the myriad of distractions along the way. They stubbornly refuse to accept *good* when they know *great* is within their reach. They accept the profound challenge of moving from conflict to health because they understand the strength and sustainable success that will follow.

There are authors who inspire me, such as Stephen Covey, Peter Drucker, Daniel Pink, and Marcus Buckingham, because their thinking resonates with me. These authors all write about things I have been thinking, and they reinforce my beliefs, giving me more courage in my work serving leaders.

Then, there are authors who challenge my thinking. They say, "Wait a minute, I don't agree with the current thinking regarding this subject. I think we are missing something and it is important!" Andy is this kind of author. You can't read this book without being challenged—challenged in your assumptions about conflict and challenged in your assumptions about what it takes to become an extraordinary team. Andy confronts much of the current thinking on these topics, yet not as a fatalist. He shows a better pathway that can create both extrinsic and intrinsic rewards, thereby allowing for more sustainable performance. This is a book to be read slowly, reflectively, and most effectively, as a community.

Andy has combined his intellectual acumen with personal experience and a deep passion for "what ought to be" to write something fresh, insightful, and loaded with potential! Oliver Wendall Holmes wrote, "The mind of man, once stretched by a new idea, can never return to its original dimensions." Get ready. You are about to go through some stretching exercises!

**Ron Price**
Executive Coach and Founder of Price Associates
January, 2014

# NEW SUGGESTED TERMS

*(a glossary of terms to move team language and culture)*

*Tribal (team and organizational) culture is created in large part by language. The following is a brief glossary of terms that can be incorporated into the vocabulary of healthy teams pushing back entropy through conflict prevention and team building:*

| | |
|---|---|
| **Alignment** | The right person doing the right things; the result of properly connecting individual talent patterns and experience with the corresponding key results for the sake of the team. |
| **Ambivert** | Someone who is in the middle of the introvert–extrovert continuum. |
| **Arbitration** | Third-party (binding or nonbinding) process that uses an arbitrator to make a ruling after hearing evidence from both sides. |
| **Attachment Style** | The way in which we tend to connect or disconnect with our significant others described with four primary styles: secure, avoidant, anxious, or ambivalent. |
| **Attack** | The direct or indirect assault on a devalued opponent. |
| **Behavioral Style** | According to our DISC profile, "how" we tend to behave. |
| **Character** | The foundational quality of healthy teams consisting in the combination of emotional intelligence and ethics. |
| **Clarity** | The ability to see and understand clearly; the absence of ambiguity. |

| | |
|---|---|
| Cohesion | The bonding, connection, or attachment of individuals to each other; the glue that holds relationships together. |
| Compelling Purpose | The big picture of "why" we exist as a team or organization; our lofty goal. |
| Conflict (interpersonal) | Committing direct or indirect attacks, resulting in substantive, relational, or personal damage against those we have devalued. We devalued them through the use of defense mechanisms and/or according to our evil intent as a result of a perceived hindrance or denial of our rightful demand. |
| Conflict Intervention | Escalating strategies used to restore relational, material, and personal damages that have resulted from conflict. |
| Conflict Prevention | Escalating strategies used to prevent relational, material, and personal damages that result from conflict. |
| Consequences | The outcomes that follow our action or inaction. |
| Core Business Definition | A clear statement that reminds us what we do, what business we are in. |
| Deep Change | Derived from Robert Quinn, the change that only comes in the form of a crisis that frees us from the status quo. |
| Devaluation | A way of reducing someone's value or dignity through the use of evil or defense mechanisms. |
| Disagreement | An aspect of diversity; two or more people seeing things differently; having different thoughts, opinions or ideas; a healthy trait of cohesive teams. |
| Dissonance | The pain that comes from holding two contradictory thoughts at the same time (e.g., "conflict is a good thing" and "conflict is a bad thing"). |
| Diversity | The healthy variety of unique personal traits and abilities all around us. |
| Dyadic | Two people working things out with each other. |

| | |
|---|---|
| **Emotional Intelligence (EQ)** | An acumen developed as we mature that allows us to be fluent and skilled in both intrapersonal and interpersonal emotional aspects of self and relationships with others. |
| **Empathy (EQ)** | Rightly interpreting what someone else is feeling and entering into the feeling with them. |
| **Entropy** | The law (principle) that describes the way everything around us (including interpersonal relationships) tends to move toward destruction or disintegration. |
| **Ethics** | Doing the right thing in accordance with an appropriate, objective, and authoritative code or standard. |
| **Evil, Human** | The propensity to intentionally cause harm to others. |
| **Extroversion** | An outgoing, gregarious approach to life that acts rather than reacts. |
| **Family of Origin** | The family you were born or adopted into as a child. |
| **Flow** | Exceptional moments in our lives where everything is harmonious, where results seem effortless and occur naturally with little effort. |
| **Groupthink** | (1) An unhealthy communication pattern that develops in an unhealthy system where the group shares a collective mind and the clear thinking of each individual is sacrificed for the common thought of the group.<br><br>(2) A force that occurs in teams that have fear-based inferior bonds of cohesion where team members do not challenge the thoughts or ideas of the team leader. |
| **Healthy Team Model** | A fivefold model of healthy teams that includes shared character, strong cohesion, laser clarity, clear communication, and positive consequences. |
| **Homeostasis** | Similar to status quo, the place the system tries to go back to; the default or normal setting. |

| Identified Patient (IP) | A family systems theory term referring to the person in the family system that carries the symptoms of the family dysfunction; this person is the one the family sends to therapy as the "problem," the scapegoat. |
|---|---|
| Incivility | Seemingly small breeches in workplace norms that break down team cohesion and clarity. |
| Interpersonal | Between people. |
| Intrapersonal | Inside the individual. |
| Introversion | An inward orientation in those who tend to move more slowly and carefully as they react to life. |
| Job Benchmark | A profile of the traits that will best meet the demands of a given position; an objective standard to measure applicants against for fit. |
| Key Results | The three to five things that will equate to success in our roles. |
| Litigation | A lawsuit brought against an opponent; something to avoid at all costs unless absolutely necessary as a last resort. |
| Mediation | A third-party process that assists two disagreeing parties to resolve their dispute. |
| Misunderstanding | Typically due to lacking information or misinformation, a wrong evaluation of the facts of a situation that can often be improved through clarification. |
| Motivation (EQ) | The ability to persist and stay motivated in the midst of adversity; the ability to be motivated apart from a carrot or a stick. |
| Motivation 2.0 or 2.1, Extrinsic | From Daniel Pink, Drive—the old school method of motivating employees with reward and punishment (carrot and stick); 2.1 = doing the same thing but with less rigidity in the environment. |
| Motivation 3.0, Intrinsic | From Daniel Pink, Drive—the new way of understanding the superior nature of intrinsic motivation in the workplace (especially with more creative, nonrepetitive tasks). |
| Motivator, Workplace | One of six primary drives that explains "why" we do what we do (carrot or stick motivation). |

| Organization | An entity comprised of people gathered to achieve a common objective that relies heavily on structure, order, and management. |
| --- | --- |
| Personal Damage | Unseen emotional and psychological damage done to the target of interpersonal conflict through a direct or indirect attack. |
| Reciprocity | Treating people as we would like to be treated; sharing what we have with others on the team. |
| Relational Damage | Damage to the relationship between two parties due to conflict. |
| Resistance | Using the two sides of character (EQ and Ethics) to resist our propensity toward evil, defense mechanisms, and devaluing others. |
| Respect | Valuing others as human beings who have inherent worth and dignity. |
| Responsibility | The antidote to the bad excuse of humanness. |
| Restraint | Holding ourselves back; not demanding our way. |
| Role Clarity | A clear understanding of who we are, our strengths and talents, and the key results we are pursuing on the team. |
| Self-Awareness (EQ) | Being aware of my own emotional state correctly labeling what I am feeling, and why. |
| Self-Regulation (EQ) | The ability to come back to a calm (nonemotionally aroused) state in less time. |
| Social Intelligence | The way we cocreate each other (for better or worse) due to our neural wiring to connect and influence each other. |
| Social Skills (EQ) | The ability to successfully manage relationships around me, including my emotions and the emotions of others. |
| Status Quo | The way things are; the way they have always been; the system's normal. |
| Stressor | Something either inside the individual, in the relationship, or in the environment that imposes strain or stress. |

| Substantive Damage | The harm caused in an indirect or direct conflict attack against an opponent; material (financial, property, reputation, or other) damage. |
|---|---|
| System | An interconnected group of individuals that mutually influences and affects one another and the whole. |
| Team, General | An identifiable, rightly sized, organized, and interconnected group of members that operates according to certain team rules and pursues common objectives. |
| Team, Healthy | An identifiable, rightly sized, well-organized, and strongly interconnected group of securely attached members in vital relationship with each other. They share common tribal language, culture, core values, and beliefs and operate in accordance with them; they clearly understand individual and group roles and core purposes that together cocreate positive consequences of all sorts. |
| Triadic | Three people working it out. |
| Tribe | A group of people who share common beliefs, values, and culture and are led by tribal leaders. |
| Values, Aspirational | What we would like to be like as a team. |
| Values, Core | The two or three values most important for the team. |
| Values, Practiced | How we actually behave as a team. |
| Willful Blindness | A legal term that refers to people who should or could know and refuse to see. |

# OUR ADDITIONAL TRIBAL TERMS:

*(Insert your own teams' terms that are part of your culture of health here.)*

# PROLOGUE

# THE PLAYING FIELD

*The field isn't level.* No matter how hard we try to convince our-selves that it is or should be, the stark reality of a sloped field stares us in the face. The field naturally inclines away from health, functionality, productivity, and profit and gravitates in-stead toward disease, dysfunction, nonproductivity, and loss. This would seem to be quite a negative note to begin a book on organizational health. Do you see the world this way? Or do you hold with many positive thinkers that things naturally improve, that to prosper all we need to do is get out of the way, let nature take its course, and do nothing? Is the field level? Is it inclined toward health? Or is it sloped notably toward failure and conflict by the principle of entropy?

In an unlevel world, conflict prevention and team building are two sides of the same coin. They are inseparable and deeply interconnected aspects of a joint solution to the problem of a sloped playing field. *To do nothing is to do something.* This princi-ple can readily be seen in interpersonal relationships of all sorts. A marriage that is not nurtured and cared for does not inher-ently or passively tend toward closeness and intimacy. Parents who neglect to spend time (quality or quantity) with their kids will almost certainly experience a loss rather than a connection with them. Teammates who do not intentionally focus on developing team health will not miraculously or spontaneously stumble onto it.

The natural world also operates according to this same principle. Things neglected (not maintained through the addition of outside energy) tend toward disorder and disintegration, not toward order and harmony. The natural outcome of failing to maintain our car, our house, our computer is predictable. In the science world, this is called the law of entropy, the second law of thermodynamics. The law is inviolable and yet, we persist in deluding ourselves that this principle does not hold true in the life cycle and health of our organization or team. Organizations and the teams that comprise them (like human beings, the world around them, and interpersonal relationships) do not naturally or automatically incline toward health.

## YOUR TEAM

We commonly read books or hear presentations about team dysfunction and fail to connect the dots to our own situation. We tell ourselves that our teams are fine and it's not that bad where we work. We disconnect from the reality around us. That's how it is for Pat, a hygienist at a local dental practice. She regularly experiences stress from a lack of organizational health at the office. She comes home from work with residual frustration and is short with the kids. One of the dentists makes her fearful at times, and she doesn't know how to talk to him. He has a certain presence that seems to evoke anxiety in her. These feelings affect her morale and engagement every day. Now it is affecting her personal life as well. She is convinced that she cannot talk to the dentist about the way she feels because things won't change anyway.

Steve, a contruction manager, has worked in the same organization for fourteen years and was promoted as a partner two years ago. The company has grown and done quite well financially during his years of service. He and the other three partners, though, have noticed an increasing turnover among their project managers and they don't understand why. Steve's team is showing some serious signs of ill health, but no one in leadership wants to admit it. He realizes that they need to do something fast to stop the revolving exit door. Steve sometimes reads articles about organizational health and conflict reduction and dreams of implementing some of the strategies he reads about. In the end, however, it seems like the company is never going to change. Steve has resigned himself to the status quo.

What about your team? Just as it was in Pat's office and in Steve's company, it is highly probable that many of the symptoms of conflict and indicators of ill health discussed in this book are present in your team. Entropy happens everywhere and in every organization. Yours included. None of us is exempt.

It is increasingly argued that organizational health is the most important factor in a company. Health, as the foundation, underlies all other sought-after results. Accordingly, it needs to be our primary focus, even more than other commonly stated organizational goals. More than profits? Other tangible results? The answer is a resounding yes. Organizational health leads to all of these outcomes. Without it, we may be profitable but miss the intrinsic satisfaction and sense of purpose that our work life is intended to bring.

Health is the horse in front of the cart of additional positive re-sults. Many companies are awakening to the central importance of this factor. If organizational health is, in fact, the most impor-tant thing, we would expect to see a central, clear, and unified priority in organizations toward its cultivation and maintenance. Sadly, for many companies, this is not the case. The time and budget commitment to meaningful growth and health-produc-ing experiences for individuals and teams is an afterthought at best, a mere footnote on the calendar and the annual budget, lost in the fine print at the footer of the page.

It has been estimated that world-class corporations spend at a minimum 5–10 percent of employee payroll on growth and de-velopment.[1] Why? Because the playing field is not level. It is far easier for a team to slide toward inevitable conflict and ill health than to do the often arduous, though surprisingly pleasurable, work required to move uphill toward team vitality. However, hard work is worth it. Investing in team health pays manifold dividends.

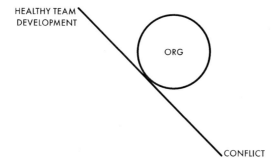

**Figure 1.** The downhill slope toward conflict.

1 This statistic is taken from the Odyssey Transformational Strategies training pro-gram as created by the late John Butler (recorded in Ron Price's personal notes).

Sometimes a picture says a thousand words. This is a main premise of this book: it's easier to go backwards than forwards, downhill than uphill.

**Sliding toward conflict is natural, and moving away from conflict towards healthy team development requires sustained energy and focus.**

# THE DESIGN OF THIS BOOK

This book is designed as a field manual for living life in an un-level world. It is created to be used in a coaching relationship (though it will prove helpful in other contexts) as a place where key principles and concepts are kept within easy access and proximity. The key principles in this small volume, though pursued over the course of a lifetime, will never be fully mastered. There will always be room for improvement.

I hope you have received this book from someone in a position to help you grow toward your fullest potential self. My hope is that its contents, as part of a nurturing relationship, will assist you in becoming a fully engaged member who will be part of moving the team into a whole new paradigm. Mark it up and wear it out (all but chapter 6, that is). Chapter 6 on Conflict Intervention is included as a bit of a scared-straight tactic, showing you and your team what lies ahead if you all are not willing to get on board with pursuing team health and conflict prevention together. I hope you read that chapter once and don't have to go back to it (which means the rest of the book is in play for your team).

This book is connected explicitly and implicitly throughout to the assessment model I use with my coaching clients. In particular, the discussion includes a basic familiarity with three levels of individual talent and developmental patterns: behavioral style, core motivators, and emotional intelligence, all of which are measured in the TTI Trimetrix EQ™. If you're not familiar with these sciences, I suggest that you read appendices A, B, and C before you continue. Better yet, contact me or another TTI value-added associate to find out how to take the assessment and obtain a personal report. These sciences are foundational to the understanding of interpersonal conflict and healthy team development.

If this challenge of entropy is clearly our reality, why wouldn't we accept this principle and agree to persistently work together to push uphill toward mutual success? The first obstacle, it appears, is ourselves. We've met the enemy and it is us. We first need to overcome our own psychological defenses. We quite naturally suppress topics we would rather not think about from our conscious awareness. Conflict, one of these topics, needs to be acknowledged and understood before we can begin to work against it.

So, we begin our journey toward greater team health and away from conflict. We're moving uphill from this point forward. I hope you've got good shoes for traction, have stretched, and are ready to go.

# PART 1

## MOVING AWAY FROM CONFLICT

# INTRODUCTION

# A TOPIC WE WOULD RATHER AVOID

My grandmother lived with us for several years as I was growing up. She was one of my best friends. She taught me all the ins and outs of canasta. She loved game shows. One of our favorite shows to watch on a sleepy summer morning was *The $25,000 Pyramid*. The show was hosted by, then young and ruggedly handsome, Dick Clark. Two celebrities would team up with two regular folks in pairs. In each twosome, one would give clues and the other would receive them. The basic rule was that the person giving clues could not say the word or a form of the word. Other than that, anything was fair game. The team that guessed the most words out of a possible twenty-one in the three rounds was declared the winner and went to what was called the "winner's circle."

In the winner's circle, the celebrity guest would give the clues and the contestant would receive. There were six categories to be correctly guessed. If the contestant correctly identified all six in sixty seconds, they would win the twenty-five thousand dollars. In the winner's circle the rules would tighten a little bit. The celebrity giving the clues could only list things that fit the category. Imagine yourself as the contestant on *The $25,000*

*Pyramid.* Your celebrity partner begins to list the following: death, taxes, dysfunctional families, conflict. You quickly think, *bad things, things that are inevitable, things that are uncomfortable, things that are painful, things we don't want to think about, things we deny or at least pretend to.*

Death, though an eventual reality for all of us (and a ready example of entropy), is something most of us walk around pretending doesn't exist.[2] We actively suppress our awareness of this indisputable fact. On a lesser level, taxes are something most of us try not to think about more than once a year. We procrastinate gathering our information, filling out our returns, and writing checks (if we owe taxes). Dysfunctional family systems thrive on this same principle of denial. What dysfunction? Not *our* family! Other families may have problems but not *ours.* So also it is with conflict. We expend massive amounts of internal energy seeking to suppress the awareness of its existence and impact on our lives. *We are deeply conflicted about conflict.* Listen to how Margaret Heffernan described this reality under what she referred to as the "ostrich effect":

> We all recognize the human desire at times to prefer ignorance to knowledge and to deal with conflict and change by imagining it out of existence. . . . It's more than just wishful thinking. In burying our heads in the sand, we are trying to pretend the threat doesn't exist and that we don't have to change. We are also trying hard to avoid conflict: If the threat's not there, I don't have to fight it. A preference for the status quo, combined with an aversion to conflict, compels us to turn a blind eye to problems and conflicts we just don't want to deal with.[3]

---

2 This is the subject of Ernest Becker's *The Denial of Death.*

3 Margaret Heffernan, *Willful Blindness: Why We Ignore the Obvious at Our Peril* (New York: Walker & Co., 2011), 87.

One of my favorite movies is M. Night Shamalyn's *The Village*. In the story, a puritanical village is surrounded by woods in which "those we don't speak of" dwell. The village is controlled through the use of this fear of the unknown woods dwellers. Fear is a powerful and primeval motivator. The fact that conflict is usually an undiscussed subject is reflective of our innate anxiety about it. Though the experts have tried to convince us in our heads of the goodness of conflict, our guts inform us otherwise. In Part 1, you are invited into an awkward conversation that you might rather prefer not to have. Nonetheless, entering the conversation opens new doors to health in all aspects of our lives.

We want to attempt to understand what conflict is, where it comes from, and what we can do about it. What we do know is that conflict is taking a huge toll on the organizations, families, and institutions we are a part of. And yet, this large problem in organizations and the teams that comprise them is often suppressed from our collective and individual conscious awareness. This team-killing dynamic is pushed out of sight, but not out of existence. Pretending it's not there doesn't put this boogeyman back into the closet.

Defense wins championships. Offense scores points and is often perceived as more glamorous. I remember watching Billy "White Shoes" Johnson, a wide receiver for the Houston Oilers, do his touchdown dance. All eyes in the stadium fixed on him as he performed his signature moves, complete with his trademark white shoes. Offense gets notoriety, but most sports experts would agree defense wins championships. So, we begin not with offense (team building) but with defense. Conflict prevention begins with an understanding of its origin and development.

# 1

## PEOPLE ARE DIFFERENT

People are people; why should it be that you
and I should get along so awfully?

### — Depeche Mode

People are people. Yet no two people are alike. Like snowflakes, we all share remarkable similarity as human beings (all snowflakes are cold and white), and yet we embody a robust individual distinctiveness (no two snowflakes are the same). There are no clones, except in bad sci-fi movies. Each person on the planet is a collection of many levels or layers of uniqueness, ways in which each story is truly one of a kind.

One of the most common responses to "what is conflict?" is that it relates to our differences. We conflict, says this theory, because we differ. The reality of diversity and differences is undeniable. The world around us is filled with a rich and wonderful variety. Whether these differences can be proven to be the cause of conflict remains to be seen. We begin, however, by observing that these differences are of three different sorts: the hand we're dealt (things we didn't choose), things that are a mixture of fate and our responses (things we, with possible limitations, had some choice in), and things we choose. As Ron Price, one of my significant mentors, taught me years ago, a life lived well can be summed up under the philosophy: *know yourself, choose yourself, create yourself, give yourself.*[4] We begin with knowing ourselves and others, understanding the differences.

# THE HAND WE'RE DEALT

For all of us, there are certain things we don't get to choose. Numerous things are chosen for us, and we receive the hand we're dealt. There doesn't seem to be any rhyme or reason to this distribution. We grasp in the dark for answers to why. It appears to be rather random, even arbitrary, and we hope or even pray that it is not capricious. Mihaly Csikszentmihalyi [*six-cent-mu-haley*] agreed:

> Whether we like it or not, each of us is constrained by limits on what we can do and feel. . . . How a person lives depends in large part on sex, age, and social position. *The accident of birth* puts a person in a slot that greatly determines what sorts of experiences his or her life will consist of. . . . Unfortunately there is no justice, nor any rhyme or reason, in one person being born into a starving community, perhaps even with a congenital physical defect, while another starts life with good looks, good health, and a large bank account."[5]

Some people attribute this assignment to fate, others to God, and many of us resist the notion of determinism of any kind altogether. Whether we acknowledge it or not, the fact remains that there are many things in our lives that we did not choose. Think about the following.

---

4 "Know yourself" is most often first attributed to Socrates; "Choose yourself" is the theme of Soren Kierkegaard; "Create yourself" is attributed to Mirandola; "Give yourself" is the philosophy of Jesus Christ and others.

5 Mihaly Csikszentmihalyi, *Finding Flow: The Psychology of Engagement with Everyday Life* (New York: Basic Books, 1997), 5–7 (italics added).

## AGE

We are as old as we are, at any given moment. We can't control it. Though we try to slow its progress, or at least the appearance of its progress, age is a key aspect of each one of us. In reality, we are all advancing toward our eventual demise, moving slowly or rapidly, but surely nonetheless toward our eventual mortality (entropy at work). In addition, as we age, we tend to move further away ideologically and culturally from those who are younger, creating a potential generation gap. How much conflict is connected to this ever-developing chasm? Different generations continue to misunderstand and condemn one another in the same way that they have for thousands of years.

## GENDER

I'm male. I didn't think it was all that significant until I was in my early forties going through a counseling program and learning about feminist theory for the first time. What a shock to realize that I was part of a privileged class called male. Since then, I have come to understand much more deeply the great divide between the genders, not only in the United States, but around the world. Gender matters. Here again, we don't choose our gender, it is issued to us.

## RACE

We are all one of the categories (or a mixture of several) on the college admission application. We each have a racial or ethnic background and a cultural heritage that, in part, defines us. We identify, even by not identifying, with a particular race or with a mix of races that are part of our internal composition, our DNA. To understand the impact of race on conflict, we don't have to look far. Think of the implication of being Jewish during the regime of the Third Reich. Think of the implication of being black in the American South. Think of the implication of being Tutsi or Hutu, of being Serbian or Croatian, of being Arab or Jew. And yet, this aspect of self is not chosen, but rather assigned to us at birth.

## PHYSICAL TRAITS

Some of us are more beautiful than others as viewed through the current cultural lens of beauty. For some periods of history, fat was in. For others, the anorexic model is the stereotype to which women aspire. Tallness ... shortness ... baldness ... green eyes ... black hair or red. Beauty is in the eye of the beholder, and yet the culture all around us seeks to influence our thinking about what is beautiful. Though we can all work at physical fitness or be surgically altered, there still remain physical traits that are unalterable. We get the physical traits we were born with.

## HEALTH

Good health is a tremendous blessing. Those of us who enjoy it often take it for granted. Though some diseases or injuries are the result of personal neglect, many have nothing whatsoever to do with our choices. Science continues to identify with greater accuracy genetic markers that indicate the potential for life-threatening diseases. Here again, it seems we are often given a gift of health or a health-related challenge that we have not earned.

## INTELLIGENCES

We are all born with a certain amount of smarts, an IQ if you will. Thankfully, we can work hard in school to make ourselves more knowledgeable in many areas. The fact remains, however, that we each possess a differing and limited amount of inborn intelligence. Our job is to utilize ours to the utmost and to develop, to its maximum potential, our capacity according to our IQ.

As subcategories of overall intelligence, we are all also given differing levels of other intelligences. Howard Gardner identified seven different types of intelligence and corresponding learning styles: visual–spatial, bodily–kinesthetic, musical, interpersonal, intrapersonal, linguistic, logical–mathematical. These different types of intelligence similarly can only be developed on the basis of the initial gifting we receive.

## FAMILY OF ORIGIN

You didn't get to choose your parents or the extended family clan to which you were connected. You and I can choose how we interact with relatives, but we don't get to choose the people with whom we share genetic or family lineage. When you were born or adopted into your family system, you also inherited a long history of family functionality or dysfunctionality. This arguably most powerful of shaping forces in our early lives was assigned to us.

## SOCIOECONOMIC STATUS

Our starting point is relevant. Where we begin is relevant to our eventual station in life. It is not simply the case that anyone can become anything they desire. There are legitimate limitations on one hand and advantages on the other. People from dire backgrounds can become highly successful. The fact remains, though, that we did not get to choose the economic station in life into which we were born. The starting line is uneven.

## RELIGIOUS BACKGROUND

Your family, as you arrived on the scene, had either some religious background or was nonreligious. Once you came into the family, the question became one of accepting or rejecting the family tradition. This is not easy for any of us. The pressure to conform to familial expectations in order to be accepted as a bonafide member of this key and primary social group is overwhelming. For this reason, most of us have some connection (whether a positive affirming one or a negative rejecting one) to the religious and philosophical background into which we were born.

## EARLY CHILDHOOD EXPERIENCES

Pat Benatar once sang, "hell is for children." Children are the innocent victims of varying forms of neglect, mistreatment, and abuse. They suffer at the hands of adults from which they are powerless to protect themselves. Early life experiences, particularly traumatic ones, shape our neural pathways and affect us throughout life. Children, who would never have chosen to be treated in these ways, are nonetheless victims of the evil, mental illness and selfishness of others.[6]

Many parents were themselves parented by caregivers who were impaired in various ways. Family dysfunction begets family dysfunction. Whether experiencing family dysfunction, neglect, or abuse, or receiving the nurture as children that sets us up for psychological success later in life, we had no choice in these things either.[7]

---

6 The ACE (Adverse Childhood Experiences) study is a nationwide study that looks at associations between childhood maltreatment and later-life health and well-being. For more information, see acestudy.org.

7 Fortunately, the attachment theory community informs us that "good enough" parenting is needed, not perfect parenting.

# A MIXED BAG

Other things that make us different seem to be a mixture of fate and choice, of nature, nurture, and other unknown factors. The following things appear to be the result of some inborn traits in combination with developmental experiences and choices. They all fall short of being purely conscious choices we make.

## BEHAVIORAL STYLE

This is something we can readily identify in each individual. Each of us is a combination of four behavioral continuums (DISC).[8] "DISC is the universal language of observable human behavior."[9] We're not quite sure how much of who we are behaviorally is attributable to nature or nurture.

> A person's behavior is a necessary and integral part of who they are. In other words, much of our behavior comes from "nature" (inherent), and much comes from "nurture" (our upbringing).[10]

Our behavioral style, how we interact with others and the world around us, is an intrinsic part of who we are. All 384 basic possible patterns on the DISC are right (behavioral styles in themselves are values neutral); that is, they provide much needed behavioral aspects (strengths) to the teams and groups we are a part of.

Behavioral styles are some of the most obvious ways in which we differ. They likely have some genetic components and are also the result of our development. Once they are established, however, they are fairly consistent over our life span (unless we

---

8 For an introduction to the DISC, see appendix A: Behavioral Styles (How).

9 Bill Bonstetter and Judy Suiter, *The Universal Language DISC: A Reference Manual* (Scottsdale, AZ: Target Training International, 2009), 3.

10 Ibid., 6.

experience traumatic events). Behavioral style, like bark on the outside of a tree, is an observable difference between us.

## MOTIVATORS AND PERSONAL VALUES

The motivators that drive our behaviors are not readily observed. Instead, they must be identified by deeper investigation below the surface. Where people invest their time, resources, and money points us to their values or motivators.[11] These subconscious values or beliefs are formed over time in an environment of both positive and negative events. Like behavioral styles, personal motivators seem to be a mix of both nature and nurture.

> It's like a computer's hard drive loaded with data. Where does the data come from to create our beliefs? Primarily it comes from the outside world through our senses—seeing, hearing, touching, tasting, and smelling. Where else could the data come from? It is possible that we are born with a certain amount of data already on the "hard drive."[12]

These values remain fairly constant over our life span, unless we experience significant life-changing or traumatic events. The one notable exception to this rule involves the way in which a motivator that is fulfilled loses its power to drive future behavior.[13]

---

11 For an introduction to motivators, see appendix B: Motivators (Why).

12 Bill Bonstetter, *If I Knew Then: How to Take Control of Your Career and Build the Lifestyle You Deserve* (Scottsdale, AZ: Target Training International, 1999–2008), 13.

13 Bill Gates is an example of this. He "filled up" to a large extent his utilitarian drive (how much money does one need?). We then saw that drive decrease and his social drive increase, resulting in the Bill and Melinda Gates Foundation.

# ATTACHMENT STYLE

It is believed that attachment styles are developed in early childhood. Attachment figures, generally mom and dad, are experienced by the child as either a safe base or as unsafe, unavailable, or even unreliable. Corresponding to the parental style, the child develops an attachment pattern that is characteristically one of four basic styles: *secure, avoidant, anxious,* or *ambivalent.*[14]

The securely attached child has confidence that the attachment figure (object) will remain available (even creating an internalized representation of the object). Because of this perceived safety, he or she is free to venture away from the parent and explore the world. If the parent is experienced as absent (emotionally or physically), the child will often initially experience anxiety. This is exemplified in the cries of the infant in the absence of its mother. If the child gets "stuck" in this mode, it forms an anxious attachment style. At some point, the child will become weary of crying out (protesting) and give up seeking the caregiver's return. This becomes an avoidant, or shut down, attachment style. An unpredictable, neglectful, or abusive parent will often create a reciprocating pattern between these two extremes of avoidance and anxiety in the child, the ambivalent attachment style.

If we were fortunate enough to be born to emotionally healthy and available parents, we may have inherited a secure attachment style. If not, our only choice in early childhood was to determine how we would cope with their unavailability.

---

14 These attachment styles have been proven to be a significant aspect of our romantic relationships. They also impact other relationships, including our relationships with others on the team.

## INTROVERSION / EXTROVERSION

There is a quiet revolution that is beginning to spread.[15] Western culture in America that has been extremely biased toward extroversion is being challenged. The status quo is being questioned by many introverts who are growing aware that they are not alone and feel emboldened to step forward and let their contrary ideas be known. Susan Cain, a thought leader in this area, is leading the way, beginning with her ground-breaking work *Quiet: The Power of Introverts in a World That Can't Stop Talking.*

We are in the midst of nothing less than a possible paradigm shift. At the beginning of the twentieth century, we shifted from what Warren Susman called a Culture of Character to a Culture of Personality.[16] There is emerging evidence that we are moving back toward the cultural idea of character as foundational because of the growing influence of introverts, who comprise one-half of the population.

---

15  For an ongoing discussion of introversion as it relates to leadership and other related workplace and team-related topics, see my personal blog at www.introvertrevolution.com.

16  Susan Cain, *Quiet: The Power of Introverts in a World That Can't Stop Talking* (New York: Crown, 2012), 21.

# A CULTURE OF CHARACTER
# OR A CULTURE OF PERSONALITY?

Susan Cain traced the development of a culture shift from a cultural foundation of character to one of personality and charisma. Near the turn of the twentieth century, under the influence of men like Dale Carnegie and others, we began to move toward a new ideal of self, the charismatic individual, or, as Cain called it, "the performing self."[17] The culture (or cult) of personality has continued to advance, unquestioned for the most part, and has influenced all aspects of current society.

Under the influence of leaders like Susan Cain, we are possibly beginning to awaken to a fresh understanding of this cultural drift toward extroversion at the expense of introversion. Through experiences of disappointment and disillusionment, we are beginning to rethink the stereotypes of leadership. The charismatic leader is a myth being increasingly brought under new scrutiny. These findings align with the research that has emerged from the business community reflected in the writing of Jim Collins, Peter Drucker, and others. Consider the following statement from Drucker:

> Among the most effective leaders I have encountered and worked with in half a century, some locked themselves into their office and others were ultragregarious. Some were quick and impulsive, while others studied the situation and took forever to come to a decision. . . . The one and only personality trait the effective ones I have encountered did have in common was something they did *not* have: they had little or no "charisma" and little use either for the term or what it signifies.[18]

This is a significant difference that contributes to the richness of diversity in the human race. This is also a key factor for teams and groups to be aware of as they seek to better understand

---

17 Ibid., 21.

18 Peter Drucker, quoted in Cain, *Quiet*, 53.

one another. We need both extroverts and introverts, kings and priests, warriors and sages to get the job done as a team.

## THINGS WE CAN CHOOSE

Robert Quinn contrasted the radical difference between those who choose life following the fearful path of deep change and those who opt for lives of "quiet desperation." The desperate become passive, take on a victim mentality, and become by default the "walking dead." Quinn's description of such people continues:

> They tend to experience feelings of meaninglessness, hopeless-ness, and impotence in their work roles, often taking on the role of "poor victim." A victim is a person who suffers a loss because of the actions of others. A victim tends to believe that salvation comes only from the actions of others. They have little choice but to whine and wait until something good happens. Living with someone who chooses to play the victim role is draining; working in an organi-zation where many people have chosen the victim role is abso-lutely depressing. Like a disease, the condition tends to spread. In today's organizations, many people are dying, not physically, but psychologically.[19]

The field isn't level and the starting line is uneven. Some have clear advantages in the race. Others are beginning from far behind. Wherever we began, at this point in the journey, we all have choices to make. We may have been victimized in the past, but we do not have to allow ourselves to be victimized in the present or the future. Life, by definition, involves the abil-ity to choose, an active response to life and relationships. Victor Frankl, the psychologist who notably survived the death camp at Auschwitz spoke of our ability to choose meaning in the worst of outward circumstances.

---

19 Robert Quinn, *Deep Change: Discovering the Leader Within* (San Francisco: Jossey-Bass, 1996), 21.

> Does man have no choice of action in the face of such circumstances? . . . The experiences of camp life show that man does have a choice of action. . . . Man can preserve a vestige of spiritual freedom, of independence of mind, even in such terrible conditions of psychic and physical stress.[20]

Frankl reminded us that even in the bleakest environment, we still have choices that we are able to make.

*Know yourself. Accept yourself. Then, choose yourself.* Regardless of the differences we have discussed above, we all retain the ability to determine our own destiny on many levels. It may not be as simple as "children can become anything they want to be," a thought popularized in our public school systems.[21] There are certain innate limitations on each of us. However, within or even despite those limitations, we can each reach our fullest potential and become the best version possible of ourselves. Our past, though always part of who we are, need not *define* us. There are certain aspects of us and our lives that are most definitely ours for the choosing.

## CHOSEN VIEW OF SELF

"An abnormal reaction to an abnormal situation is normal behavior."[22] Our view of self normally connects directly to our personal narrative, the story we tell ourselves of our growth and development. Many of us experienced less-than-ideal family systems, dynamics that have shaped us. We may have chosen certain coping mechanisms to survive the dysfunction. At this point, however, we each need to choose whether we will continue to allow those experiences to define us. Our view of self is foundational. It is arguable that the vast majority of time and

---

20 Viktor Frankl, *Man's Search for Meaning* (Boston: Beacon Press, 2006), 65.

21 Even with infinite practice, I could never have been Michael Jordan.

22 Frankl, *Man's Search,* 20.

money spent in therapy revolves around revising our view of self. Seeing ourselves differently is hard work. It is, however, well worth the effort.

## CHOSEN VIEW OF OTHERS

We not only choose how we see ourselves, we also choose how we view others. We are not passive victims of the influences around us. In the most difficult and devaluing contexts, we all can choose to differentiate ourselves from the masses. We can value all individuals simply for who they are. Bigotry in all its forms is based on learned ignorance and fear. Choosing to see others as inherently valuable and worthy of dignity and respect is the path toward full humanity. These two, our view of self and our view of others, are related. Many of us don't know ourselves very well, and therefore, we are rendered unable to value and understand others around us.

## LIFESTYLE (BEHAVIORS AND ATTITUDES)

In addition to our chosen view of self and others, we have meaningful choices to make about the way we will live our lives. Though we each have a particular blend of DISC traits and tendencies, within that style, we still retain the ability to choose our behavioral responses to life. Our attitude is also a choice. We can succumb to the external or internal pressure to give in or give up or we can overcome and live lives to the fullest.

> After everything is said and done, knowing all the external parameters will not allow us to predict what [our] life will be like. . . . [We have] a mind of our own with which [we] can either decide to squander [our] opportunities, or conversely overcome some of the disadvantages of [our] birth. . . . If everything was determined by the common human condition, by social and cultural categories, and by chance, it would be useless to reflect on ways to make one's life excellent. Fortunately there is enough room for personal initiative and choice to make a real difference.[23]

---

23 Csikszentmihalyi, *Finding Flow*, 7–8 (italics added).

## PHILOSOPHY / WORLDVIEW

We didn't get to choose the environment into which we were born. This environment in our family and culture included aspects of a worldview. As children, we typically did not question the prevailing worldview around us. If our parents were Democrats, we unquestioningly leaned Democratic. The same is true for Republican households. Our family and other immediate relationships imposed upon us a certain philosophy of life. It is typically in adolescence that we began to question this philosophical framework. At some point, as we continued to grow into our own individuated self, we either accepted it for ourselves as our worldview or rejected it in part or in whole for an alternative.[24] It is then that we began to choose our belief system, our worldview, and will continue to choose it throughout our lives.

## CORE COMPETENCIES (EDUCATION)

We all have the capacity to develop core competencies, which are learned and developed skills. They are not gifts or talents to be received but are the development of those natural abilities (and some unnatural ones as well) into a repertoire of useful skills contributing to the success of the team.[25]

One of the ways in which we increase our competencies in specific areas is through formalized education and other training. We all have the opportunity to put in the requisite work to

---

24 Sadly, things like misogyny and racism can be demonstrated to be the result of an indoctrinated worldview that most often has not been questioned. These views are based largely on ignorance and naiveté. They spread multigenerationally through groups and families with very little critical thinking.

25 See Ron Price and Randy Lisk, *The Complete Leader: Everything You Need to Become a High Performing Leader*. In the book and the corresponding website (www.thecompleteleader.org), Ron and Randy explore the twenty-five competencies measured by the TTI Trimetrix HD™ assessment, which can be further developed.

better ourselves in this way, which is why education is often rightly emphasized as a way to chart a new course for the future.

## OTHER MINDS

Howard Gardner spoke of five different minds that can be mastered by each individual. Two of these five, *the respectful mind* and *the ethical mind* fit nicely into the description of character in this volume. The other three are capacities we can choose to develop over time.

> *The disciplined mind* has mastered at least one way of thinking—a distinctive mode of cognition that characterizes a specific scholarly discipline, craft, or profession. . . . *The synthesizing mind* takes information from disparate sources, understands and evaluates that information objectively, and puts it together in ways that make sense to the synthesizer and also to other persons. . . . Building on discipline and synthesis, *the creating mind* breaks new ground. It puts forth new ideas, poses unfamiliar questions, conjures up fresh ways of thinking, arrives at unexpected answers.[26]

These five minds can be chosen as areas of focus for personal development.

## CHARACTER

Character is a choice. Regardless of our background, we have the innate ability to choose whom we will become in regard to our character. We choose whether we will grow and develop or remain as we are. Character development inherently involves discipline and hard work.[27] It forms the foundation of both conflict prevention and healthy teams and is the combination of two interrelated areas of personal maturity.

---

26  Howard Gardner, *Five Minds for the Future* (Boston: Harvard Business Press, 2008), 3.

27  Chapter 8 focuses on this chosen trait.

## Emotional Intelligence (EQ)

Emotional intelligence, the ability to understand and wisely manage our own and others' emotions, is closely aligned with the concept of maturity. Children and adolescents, by default, do not typically possess high levels of emotional intelligence, which develops over time and in response to adverse experiences. We learn this skill through focus and diligence.[28]

## Ethics

From early childhood, boys and girls are trained to discern right from wrong. Our nature as human beings is intrinsically ethical in nature. Though we try to suppress our conscience, it resists suppression and continues to call us to higher standards of behavior.

These two, emotional intelligence and ethics, combine to form what we refer to as character. Character, as a function of brain development, can be formed in both the front of our brains (our rational neocortex) and the base of our brains (the emotional limbic system). More on this to come.

## WE ARE DIFFERENT

We have briefly surveyed some of the ways people differ from one another. With this complex diversity in backgrounds and experiences, it is remarkable that we ever get along. These differences are often unfairly blamed as the reason for the existence of conflict. If only we were more homogenous, more uniform, this theory implies, conflict would find no warrant to exist. This

---

28 See appendix C: Emotional Intelligence.

theory of diversity is only one of the commonly understood causes of conflict.

**Table 1.** Three Areas of Personal Differences

| THINGS WE'RE DEALT | A MIXED BAG | THINGS WE CHOOSE |
|---|---|---|
| • Age | • Behavioral Style | • View of Self |
| • Gender | • Motivators (Drives) | • View of Others |
| • Race | • Attachment Style | • Lifestyle / Attitude |
| • Physical Traits | • Introversion / Extroversion / Ambiversion | • Philosophy / Worldview |
| • Health | | • Core Competencies / Education |
| • Intelligences | | • Other Minds |
| • Family of Origin | | • Character (Ethics & EQ) |
| • Socioeconomic Status | | |
| • Religious Background | | |
| • Early Childhood Experiences | | |

We begin with a consideration of differences, a key strength to successful teams that is often inappropriately blamed as the source of conflict among them. If it's not differences, then what is the source of the strife that hinders healthy team development and mutual success? Maybe it's disagreement.

# DISAGREEMENT

It has been my experience that many of us in America often equate the concepts of conflict and disagreement. In response to the foundational question, what is conflict? I have most often received responses that include disagreement and differences of opinion. Disagreement, however, is intrinsically tied to our diversity. We differ on many levels. People who differ as widely as we do are inevitably going to see and experience things differently, leading to inevitable disagreement. But is disagreement conflict?

# HEALTHY DISAGREEMENT

Conflict, as we will discuss it, has a negative connotation.[29] Disagreement, due to its common close association with conflict, often shares this negativity. It gets a bad rap. Disagreement is healthy among mature teams working well together. Here's how Peter Drucker explained this point:

> Dissent [*disagreement*] is constructive, provided you have unity on mission and purpose and values. When you have disagreement on values—very basic disagreement—the integrity of the organization is at stake, and critical decisions must be made.[30]

Dissent or disagreement is a positive thing when it takes place within a safe environment of shared values. In these cases, we disagree agreeably and respectfully. We disagree ideologically and do not make things overly personal. According to Drucker, however, when we disagree about core values, it is another story. As we will see, core value disagreement readily turns

---

29 Others try to reframe conflict as a positive thing.

30 Peter Drucker, *The Five Most Important Questions You Will Ever Ask about Your Nonprofit Organization: Participant's Workbook* (San Francisco: Jossey-Bass, 1993), 11 (italics added).

toward judging, devaluation, and condemnation of one another and quickly crosses the line into conflict.

**Disagreement itself is neither conflict nor a bad thing.**

## UNITY, NOT UNIFORMITY

Uniformity, the opposite pole from a healthy acceptance and embrace of diversity, attempts to make everyone agree for the sake of unity. Unity at the core of the team is based on shared mission, purpose, and values—tribal culture. Therefore, healthy disagreement in the form of nonuniform thoughts about issues frequently and naturally occurs within the unity of a healthy team or organization.

It is common to push uniformity as the answer to disagreement when disagreement is viewed as the essence of conflict. This solution seems intuitive: eliminate diversity, eliminate conflict. Ironically, it is most often conflict in various forms that is used to eliminate this perceived enemy of diversity.[31] We'll create unity, even if we need to do so by force. This can't be the answer to the problem of conflict. So where does conflict come from?

---

31 This was the unfortunate and evil strategy of the Third Reich, which sought to forcibly eliminate racial and religious diversity as a means of eliminating conflict in an effort to bring the German nation to a new period of unity and supremacy.

# 2

## CONTRIBUTORS TO CONFLICT

We're so different in so many ways. Many directly equate these inherent differences with the existence of conflict. When describing a conflict, we often say people had a difference. In other words, they are different and on the basis of those differences, they are no longer getting along. We sometimes grant divorce on the basis of these *irreconcilable differences*, these ways in which each partner in the marriage relationship is no longer able to appreciate the differences that once drew them into the relationship. But did the differences really cause the conflict? Are differences irreconcilable? Where does conflict come from? Before we can proceed, we need to address a current cultural elephant in the room, the "conflict is good" view.

## IS CONFLICT A GOOD THING?

It is a common practice for experts in various fields to suggest that things we commonly think of as negative are in reality not so. These authorities attempt to reframe our unenlightened understanding. The topic of conflict is often presented in such a light. We are informed by the so-called experts that conflict is a good thing, a constructive thing that prevents us from the negative impact of groupthink. No conflict, no real discussion of alternatives on the team.

Think of other realities that seem to be a mixture of good and bad. Is pain good? Without it we would be unaware of harm to our bodies. Congenital insensitivity to pain (CIP), also known as congenital analgesia, is a rare condition where a person cannot feel physical pain. People with CIP can easily harm themselves. So in that sense, pain, for the rest of us, is a good (useful) thing. What about suffering? Many of us would be able to describe the ways in which suffering has brought about greater character development. But does that make suffering good? Or does it rather make something that is not good, sometimes useful for a greater purpose? But what is good about conflict? Wouldn't this world and our relationships be better without it?

Instead of simply calling things that were previously called bad "good," we may want to be more careful and precise with our language here. There is a great deal of difference between goodness and related topics such as usefulness or productiveness. We may want to ask somewhat different questions. Is conflict useful? Is it productive? Depending on our definition of conflict, we may or may not be able to concede its usefulness or productiveness, but its goodness?

# THE EMPEROR'S NEW CLOTHES: THE POWER OF GROUPTHINK

In the classic Hans Christian Andersen children's story, the emperor was able to convince his court and the citizens of his kingdom of the beauty of his nonexistent clothes.[32] This is a story of the power of self-deception and groupthink. The power of the one in authority, combined with fear and unhealthy groupthink dynamics, perpetuated the myth the emperor had created.

We may have forgotten the origin of the clothes themselves. They came from what Andersen called "swindlers." These corrupt clothiers who sold the invisible clothes to the emperor for a profit were the origin of the problem. The narcissistic pride of the emperor made him a ready mark. The tailors and the emperor would have convinced the kingdom of the lie, were it not for the honesty of a young child.

So it is perhaps in our thinking about conflict. Our old clothes informed us that conflict was something bad, something to be avoided, a sign of problems, not a sign of health. But then the swindlers came and sold us a new set of clothes. I don't think the purveyors of "conflict is good" have done it with any malicious intent.[33] It is likely a result of our culture shifting toward more postmodern thinking, less black-and-white categories, which in many areas has been progress. In the arena of conflict, however, we may need to look at ourselves and our new clothes with new eyes.

---

32 An English translation of the story is included in appendix D. If you haven't read the story in a while, you can reread it now.

33 The current landscape of the business community reflects the extrovert bias of the surrounding culture. For many extroverts (high D), conflict is viewed as good, something at which to win.

It seems that we may have another example of the so-called experts intellectually bullying us into seeing things as opposite to how they first or instinctively appear. Sometimes the emperors among us, in making these bold assertions about their new clothes, are eventually found out and exposed as naked and ashamed. If conflict is indeed good, then why do almost all of us have a natural aversion to it and a corresponding revulsion?[34] If it were actually good, would our bodies give us internal clues to suggest the opposite? Sometimes, it is most healthy to go with your gut.[35] What is your gut telling you about conflict?

Cognitive dissonance is created when we attempt to hold two contradictory positions simultaneously. To reduce dissonance, we often eliminate one of the positions to reduce the pain that arises from this internal conflict. Many of us have attempted to listen to the experts, to tell ourselves that conflict really is a good thing. When our bodies (our limbic brains) tell us otherwise, we attempt to eliminate the internal dissonance with the authoritative voice of the experts. Our limbic brains know better, however, and continue to signal conflict as a threat. The confusion in our heads about the nature of conflict is driven in part by the ambiguity that is often present in the English language.

## WHAT IS CONFLICT?

Conflict, in the English language, is used to describe a wide range of things. The latest skirmish between Israel and Syria is called a conflict. Rockets are flying, tanks are rolling, people are

---

34 The behavioral styles of high I, high S, and high C are all conflict-averse. See appendix A.

35 Dissonance occurs when the frontal cortex (the rational brain) and the limbic brain (the emotional center) disagree. The appeal of so-called experts to the rational brain does not alter our instinctual belief about conflict.

dying. And we call this conflict. On the other extreme, a couple argues over what to have for dinner. She had her heart set on seafood and he was thinking Italian. The process by which they seek to share their feelings and come to a joint selection is often referred to as the couple having a conflict. Context is everything. There is great potential for misunderstanding and confusion around the English word "conflict."

If we want to have a meaningful discussion about the type of conflict we are seeking to understand in this book, *conflict proper*, we need to carefully define our terms. Let's move toward a working definition of conflict. To do that, we will look at some of the leading contenders in the field of conflict theory and evaluate them as to their respective merits. As we do so, notice that three things are inherently interconnected:

- Our working definition of conflict
- Our theory about its origin or cause
- Our philosophy of its resolution

*Problem definitions are integrally connected to problem solutions.* To understand what conflict is, we first need to understand where it is coming from. There are several commonly suggested causes of interpersonal conflict among us. We will examine them in order of logical strength.

**How we define the problem dictates our approach to solving it.**

## CONTEMPORARY THEORIES OF CONFLICT

In the marketplace of ideas today, there are several recurring theories of conflict. Though each theory has some merit, upon further consideration, each falls short of the criteria necessary for it to be labeled a rational explanation of causality. Aspects of conflict that fall short of being causal can be shown instead to be merely contributors, environmental factors:

## THE HUMANNESS THEORY

> I'm only human.
> Of flesh and blood, I'm made.
> Human.
> Born to make mistakes.

### — The Human League

This is the song from the 1980s that plays in the background of a recent ad campaign for a car insurance company. The point is that accidents happen. Therefore, you need insurance. In one of the scenes, a neighbor unthinkingly sawed off a large limb of his tree directly above a vehicle. Honestly, we can consider this an act of carelessness and stupidity. We do make mistakes, sometimes out of carelessness and other times after what we thought was careful consideration of the situation. However, is our humanity a valid excuse? In the case of the damage done by the falling limb, the gentleman who cut off the branch would be liable for the damage caused, not the neighbor who was counseled to buy the insurance.

"To err is human."[36] By the same logic, to conflict with one another is human. Very small children, without any coaching from their parents, quite naturally engage in the art of interpersonal conflict. Conflict, for human beings, comes quite instinctively and intuitively. If this is our tendency, is it our inevitable des-

---

36 Alexander Pope, *An Essay on Criticism* (London, 1711).

tiny? Are we doomed to continue in this destructive human propensity? Or is this tendency toward conflict a part of our lower nature, something we are capable of rising above?

Human beings are an interesting mix of noble and base aspects. The cartoon that pictures an angel on one shoulder and a demon on the other resonates with us. We often find ourselves torn between following our lower nature, our devilish propensity, or our higher one, our conscience that leads us toward our more ideal human aspirations. As human beings, most of us normally seek to aim for these higher standards of behavior. We readily see the benefit in reducing or eliminating conflict from all spheres of society. We have a deeply ingrained desire to see the elimination of conflict in the world leading to a corresponding peace, a sense that all is well. This is the innate sense of justice and a desire for things to be right and peaceful that reside in the human heart.

**To explain away the presence of conflict as an inevitable result of our humanity is nothing more than a bad excuse.**

Responsible human beings do not blame their lack of relational wholeness or the presence of conflict simply on their humanity. Human beings may be prone to err, but we cannot or should not use this as a standing rationale for the presence of conflict. To succumb to this temptation for a perpetual rationalization has dire societal consequences. This first theory falls short of a satisfying explanation. Our humanity cannot be used as a justification to explain the existence of interpersonal conflict among us. There must be a deeper explanation.

## THE LACK THEORY

We live in a culture of perceived scarcity. This is what researcher and author Brené Brown called the "never-enough problem."[37] She went on to describe this shared feeling.

> Scarcity thrives in a culture where everyone is hyperaware of lack. Everything from safety and love to money and resources feels restricted or lacking. We spend inordinate amounts of time calculating how much we have, want, and don't have, and how much everyone else has, needs, and wants. What makes this constant assessing and comparing so self-defeating is that we are often comparing our lives, our marriages, our families, and our communities to unattainable, media-driven visions of perfection, or we're holding up our reality against our own fictional account of how great someone else has it.[38]

Though we in the United States still live as some of the most fortunate and advantaged people on the planet, our perception is often that we lack. It is this perceived sense of scarcity that often unfairly receives the blame for the presence of conflict.

We have conflict because there is never enough. So begins the scarcity theory. Two young boys fight over the same Tonka truck at a local day care. Though the play area is filled with trucks of all sorts, the one truck in particular, the yellow dump truck, has become the sole object of their respective desires. They tug back and forth. "Mine," they say together. In fairly short order, one boy hits the other over the head with the famed Tonka. Conflict emerges. Was this skirmish over the Tonka the result of too few toys?

If only we had enough to go around. If there was no lack, there would be no conflict. Or would there? Is it necessarily the case

---

37 Brené Brown, *Daring Greatly: How the Courage to Be Vulnerable Transforms the Way We Live, Love, Parent, and Lead* (New York: Penguin Group, 2012), 24.

38 Ibid., 26.

that conflict be our sole response to our perceived lack? Can't human beings of character forego desires or suffer want and still remain free from conflict?

We don't always pursue the higher path leading toward maturity and character. We often have conflict because we protest that our individual needs aren't being met, and the only way we can conceive of to get our needs met is to "pitch a fit." There is an uncomfortable similarity between the cries of a child who protests the absence of his mother, a boy fighting for a Tonka truck, and the cries of a grown adult who protests the absence of things he feels deserving of. One problem with managing this concept involves differentiating between needs and wants. The line between them is not always clear or readily discerned. Wants often masquerade as needs. Human beings are highly adept at blurring the line.

The human heart is insatiable. Regardless of our present circumstance, we are internally propelled toward the desire for more. Capitalism is based on this premise. Advertisers understand this. It is this principle of desire they provoke when they show us the latest thing for our consumption as a culture. Madison Avenue may have helped to create this sense of lack within us, but upon closer scrutiny, the lack we perceive evaporates in light of reality. Much of our perceived scarcity is a figment of our overactive imaginations and appetites. Blaming conflict on lack, it seems, is equally less than rational.

## THE DIVERSITY THEORY

We began to discuss this concept in chapter 1. The basic problem in society is diversity. So begins the differences theory of conflict. If only we were more uniform, we would have less conflict. At one extreme, this kind of logic has underlaid evils as heinous as Nazi Germany or the equally reprehensible white supremacism in the United States. If only we could eliminate the other races, the ones that we don't understand, the ones that aren't like us, the ones we arrogantly conclude are "inferior," all would be well. Eliminating diversity is usually advocating for the creation of uniformity, valuing the one over the many.

We can quickly see the logical and moral problems with this kind of thinking. Far from being the problem, the diversity all around us is what makes life fun and exciting.

> Remember the saying, variety is the spice of life. . . . We love variety and seek out variety. . . . Variety is what makes life exciting and fun. We appreciate variety in everything—except people. . . . Isn't it interesting? That which we desire, value, and expect in animals, food, cars, clothing, flowers, houses, vacations, jewelry, and virtually everything you can imagine—we criticize in people. With people we tend to be harsher in our judgments.[39]

Diversity is not the problem.

**The problem lies in our inability to value one another, to recognize the inherent beauty of our interdependence, to work together in harmony.**

Diversity is the answer. Embracing this diversity, fully respecting the personhood, gifts, and talents of each other, is the answer. As Aretha reminded us, the answer is spelled R-E-S-P-E-C-T.

## THE DESIRE THEORY

Human beings have natural desires. Many of these desires are necessary for the preservation of our species. Abraham Maslow correctly determined that we have a hierarchy of needs.

---

39 Bonstetter, *If I Knew Then*, 5.

Consider the natural desire for food, water, companionship, sex, and so forth. All of these biological drives are part and parcel of our continued existence as living vital organisms. It would be accurate to say that to desire is human.

Desires are substantially passive things. We don't have to try to want something; we simply experience wanting it. This, again, is the fundamental understanding of those in advertising. Among the things we find ourselves wanting are some things that are obtainable and others that are not, some things that are appropriate and others that are not. Laws, thankfully, prohibit us from obtaining some of the inappropriate things we deeply desire. For the benefit of the individual and of society as a whole, we have agreed upon certain boundaries around our desires.

Most of the things that we desire are legitimate, if not noble, pursuits. We desire a good and satisfying marriage, close relationships with our children, a satisfying and rewarding career, a good education, a nice new vehicle, a great meal, and so on. The ancient Greeks known as the Stoics suggested that the answer to the good life was the elimination of desire, a state of apathy. This ancient philosophy continues to show up in various contemporary forms today. Asceticism, in any form, is not the answer. Desire isn't the core problem in most cases. With desire, the problem is often not the object but our intensity in wanting it. We have a word for this in our culture: *obsession*. To obsess is to fixate and overfocus on a desire in an unhealthy way.[40] These obsessions move from *wants* to *must haves*, and conflict begins to sprout.

---

40 The DSM (Diagnostic and Statistical Manual of Mental Disorders), published by the American Psychiatric Association, labels this obsession that affects functioning and significant relationships as obsessive compulsive disorder.

## THE THRESHOLD OF CONFLICT

None of these in themselves (humanness, lack, diversity, or desire) creates the necessity of conflict. Though they may set the stage or stack the deck in the direction of potential conflict, they are not causes. They individually and even collectively fall short of the line that marks the emergence of conflict.

Think of the illustration of fire. To build a fire, we need fuel (wood, paper, gasoline), air, and a spark. Contributors are definite factors in the combustibility of the team. Sometimes these contributing factors can be like gasoline on a fire; they can cause the situation to increase rapidly. None of these, however, are the spark that ignites the conflict into flame. We can illustrate this principle in the following way:

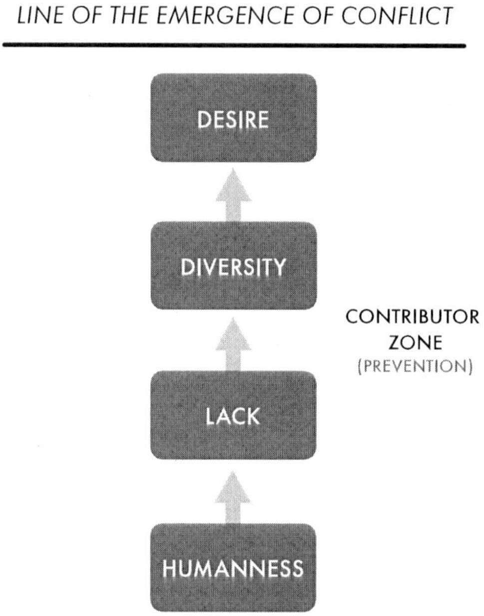

*LINE OF THE EMERGENCE OF CONFLICT*

DESIRE

DIVERSITY

CONTRIBUTOR
ZONE
(PREVENTION)

LACK

HUMANNESS

**Figure 2.** Contributors to Potential Conflict.

None of these four commonly cited reasons for the emergence and maintenance of interpersonal conflict is a necessary or sufficient cause. They may inform the situation and provide a context, an environment, where the pump is primed in the direction of conflict. One additional factor, though, remains the key to understanding the beginning of relational strife. Before we examine that key factor, there is one common misunderstanding that needs to be cleared up.

## MISUNDERSTANDINGS ARE NOT CONFLICT

There is much misunderstanding about the nature of misunderstanding. Much of what is initially understood as a conflict is more accurately described (in retrospect and with more reflection) as merely a *misunderstanding*. Communication and its counterpart, miscommunication, are always at work in interpersonal relationships. The essence of miscommunication is described simply as the failure to convey or to receive the intended message. The intended message was not correctly received. The error can be on either side and often is on both.

Misunderstanding is typically broader than miscommunication and often includes actions or inactions as well. "She didn't say 'hi' to me in the hallway today," explains the high school girl who perceives her friend's failure to greet her as intentional. Misunderstandings often include some facts or partial facts mixed with attempts to fill in gaps in the available information. What the offended high school girl doesn't realize is that her friend actually didn't see her because she was deep in thought about the final exam she was about to take.

Oftentimes, we wrongly infer motives in the midst of misunderstanding. We are often guilty of cognitive biases such as the fundamental attributional error or the self-serving bias.[41] Our reasoning on the fly is often inaccurate. We tend to default toward wrongly assessing the intent of others and as a result often take offense too easily.

## THE NEED FOR CLARIFICATION

Where there is misunderstanding, the solution is clarification. Misunderstandings are not conflicts and require a different path toward resolution. Misunderstandings are always based on some level of inaccurate information concerning words, actions, or intent. With the addition of relevant factual information, a misunderstanding is cleared up.

**Clarification is to misunderstanding as resolution is to conflict.**

It is appropriate to move tentatively into an apparent conflict situation, while looking out for the possibility of misunderstanding. Conflict proper, however, will not simply clear up with the addition of information. After all misunderstandings are clarified, a true conflict will still remain in need of resolution.

---

41 The fundamental attributional error is a result of overestimating the internal factors or personality traits of others and underestimating the external factors. We tend to consider their behavior as representative of their lack of character (internal factors) and do not explain it in light of external circumstances (as we most often do for ourselves). The self-serving bias is our way of giving ourselves credit for our successes and giving ourselves excuses for our failures based on external factors.

# PRELIMINARY DEFINITION OF CONFLICT: WHAT IT IS NOT

Conflict is not an inevitable result of being human. Human beings can resist their lower nature that leads them to conflict. Conflict is not the inevitable result of lack, scarcity, or unmet needs. People of character can endure these adverse circumstances and still refrain from conflict. Neither is conflict the product of diversity. Diversity is the spice of life and not the cause of conflict among us. Nor is it the fact that we desire. We are designed to want things. Some of the things we want aren't good for us; others are legitimate pursuits. Our desires are most definitely a mixed bag. They in themselves, however, are not the reason we find ourselves in conflict.

Conflict isn't explained away as misunderstanding either. Misunderstandings, as common as they are, require a different approach than the resolution and prevention of conflict proper. This leads us to a preliminary partial definition of conflict, defined negatively by what it is not.

**What Conflict Isn't**

- merely the result of being human,
- simply the result of lack or unmet needs,
- inevitably the product of diversity,
- necessarily the result of desire, or
- a synonym for misunderstandings.

To move toward a positive definition of conflict, we turn to a fifth factor under consideration, demand.

# 3

## WHAT DRIVES CONFLICT?

We have examined some of the most prevalent theories of conflict. We have acknowledged that indeed we are all human, that is to say imperfect; scarcity is a real problem in much of the world; the perception or reality of unmet needs causes internal emotional pain; and finally, more than all of these, the differences between us seem to be deeply related to the presence of conflict. None of these, though, has proven to be a sufficient explanation for the presence of conflict.

**Conflict seems to emerge as a consequence of not getting what we want, or as we contend in those moments, *what we deserve*.**

### EXTERNAL AND INTERNAL STRESSORS

Current theories of conflict focus heavily on external factors. The corresponding solution to conflict lies in remedying an environmental problem. This is the driving thought behind the humanness theory, the scarcity theory, and the diversity theory. Environmental factors contribute to the development of conflict by loading the situation. These factors become stressors, adding weight and challenging the capacity of individuals on the threshold of conflict.

## STRESSORS LOAD THE SITUATION

Structural design (whether a simple beam or a complex bridge) is based on an understanding of stresses, materials, and strengths. Consider the simple beam. Load is placed on the beam, which creates stress in the member, tension on the bottom, and compression on the top. If the beam has sufficient strength to handle the stress, it carries it. If it doesn't, it fails. As it is in structural design, so it is in conflict situations. People possess differing levels of strength or capacity. Related to the personal capacities of both people, relationships have combined capacities. Often, we do not see the depth of these capacities until we load the relationship.

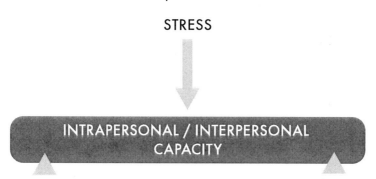

**Figure 3.** Stress loading on the individual.

Stresses added externally in the environment load or create strain in the material itself—in this case the relationship or the individual in the relationship. Any of the things discussed thus far can be stressors contributing to conflict development.

## EXTERNAL AND INTERNAL STRESSORS

Stressors that contribute to conflict come in two basic forms, external and internal. External stressors are those circumstantial or environmental variables that load the situation—contributors like humanness, perceived lack, diversity, and even healthy desires. Hidden beneath the surface of individuals involved in conflict are several types of internal stressors. Internal stressors have to do with the psychological capacity and history of the individuals involved. Every person has a past. That past is integrally connected to the nature and level of internal stress that triggers in a conflict.

Internal stressors come in two basic forms. *Vertical stress* consists of the generational loading that a person experiences in regard to their family-of-origin history and its multigenerational dysfunctional patterns. *Horizontal internal stress* has to do with the individual's capacities or incapacities to handle the current stressful situation. Both of these are in play in a highly loaded situation. Effective coaches and mediators will be attuned to all of these intrapersonal dynamics.

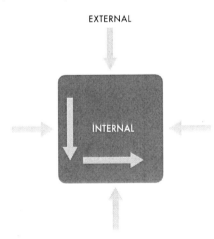

**Figure 4.** External and internal stressors in an individual.

Here are the stressors that contribute to the development of conflict:

- **External stressors** are the environmental factors or aggravations that contribute to the potential for conflict. They are *present situational* aspects, precursors, or contributors.

- **Internal horizontal stressors** are the internal factors within the individual involved in conflict situations. They are *present intrapersonal* aspects.

- **Internal vertical stressors** are the internal factors within the individual involved in conflict situations. They are *past-oriented* aspects related to *significant past relationships*.

## INTERNAL DEVELOPMENT OF CONFLICT

Conflicts begin on the inside of individuals, *intrapersonally*. Long before any outward action that signals the existence of strife, seeds that lead toward the sprouting of conflict develop within the individual. Eventually, an attack is initiated. The process emerges from the principle of desire. Desire, in itself, is not the explanation. Desires that have become elevated into demands drive the process of conflict. They are the sparks, the seeds, of the impending fire. Here's how it works.

## WHEN DESIRES BECOME DEMANDS

All human beings desire. Desire is a normal and healthy part of our existence. Sometimes, however, we desire *too much*. The marketing strategy employed by Coldstone Creamery, the ice cream shop, is clever and memorable. They offer three sizes: like it, love it, and gotta have it. In this case, we're looking at desires in a similar way. The *gotta have it desires*, a.k.a. demands, are almost always the catalyst that drives the onset and maintenance of conflict situations.

Desires usually begin small, even quite innocently. They frequently, though, do not remain small. The little voice inside us reminding us of our desire is persistent and tends to grow louder over time. That inner voice pushes us toward the principle of demand. Desire says, "I want." Demand says, "I must have." Demand is the language of must. Sometimes, as is the case in contractual obligations, our demands have justification. Often, they do not.

**In our current culture of entitlement, demands are normalized. Getting what we want is idealized.**

A demand pushes us toward the emergence of conflict, particularly when that wish is not granted.

Three key questions that begin to unpack the true nature of the conflict center on this concept. To understand the driving force underneath a current conflict situation, ask these three questions of the person on the offense:

- What do you want? (the objective)
- How much do you want it? (the size)
- What are you willing to do to get what you want? (the subjective value)

# HITTING THE WALL

Demands are resistant to opposition. They tend to move forward until they hit a wall. The wall consists of the main obstacle that is currently frustrating our ability to obtain the object of desire: the person or people of inherent value and dignity that seem to stand in the way. It is most often other people who stand between us and the object we demand.

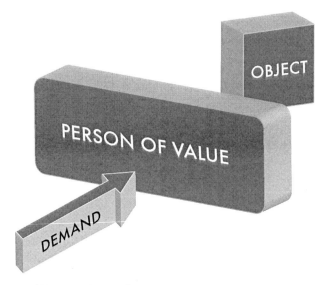

**Figure 5.** Hitting the wall.

When we hit the wall, we have an option to pause and reconsider our pursuit or, as we often choose, to move around or go through this obstacle and continue toward our desired goal. The problem with moving around the wall of our opponent by choosing conflict is that in so doing, we necessarily compromise our own character.

## PERCEIVED EGO THREAT (THWARTED DESIRES)

How do we cope with opposition, resistance, or defeat? What is our internal reaction when something we believe we ought to have been given is denied? The language of must is the language of rights, of merit, of entitlement. Though we perceive them as rights, in truth, often those things we demand are not legitimate entitlements. Perception is not reality. However, for the person driven by must, it seems to be so.

> Many people in the United States today are simply oblivious to others' needs, or, worse, think that others' needs are just not as important as their own needs [reciprocity is the inverse of this]. This state of mind is called entitlement, the pervasive belief that one deserves special treatment, success, and more material things. Entitlement is one of the key components of narcissism and one of the most damaging to others. When narcissists feel entitled to special treatment, someone invariably gets the shaft.[42]

When we do not or cannot have the thing demanded (possessions, status, power, etc.), a readily available strategy is to seek an explanation outside of ourselves for our disappointment. The thing we deserve, that to which we are entitled, is not being given to us. Someone must pay for this slight to our ego. To admit defeat, to acquiesce and go without, could bring shame and an inner sense of failure. To fight against these vulnerable feelings, we seek solutions.

## PROTECTING OURSELVES

We have a few options for responses when we encounter this kind of opposition. If we are unwilling to drop our demands, the first option we have involves protecting our ego. To do this we use defense mechanisms and often, outside of awareness, enter into familiar emotional patterns rooted in our past.

---

42 Jean Twenge and Keith Campbell, *The Narcissism Epidemic: Living in the Age of Entitlement* (New York: Free Press, 2009), 230 (italics added).

## Defense Mechanisms

Defense mechanisms are a psychological protection from a perceived ego threat. According to Gerald Corey, they "help the individual cope with anxiety and prevent the ego from being overwhelmed." The problem, however, is that in trying to lessen inner anxiety, these defenses create problems interpersonally.

**Defense mechanisms are maladaptive responses that contribute directly to the intrapersonal development of conflict.**

A defense mechanism is a form of self-deception that we use to protect ourselves from the anxiety of confronting our own weaknesses and vulnerabilities to protect our ego from feeling shame or embarrassment. Defense mechanisms that trigger in conflict situations are usually one of six common responses.

**Table 2.** Defense Mechanisms Used in Conflict[43]

| Ego Defense | Description | Implications for Conflict |
|---|---|---|
| **Projection** | Attributing to others one's own unacceptable desires and impulses | • The opponent is seen as embodying unwanted aspects of self.<br>• Our "stuff" is put onto others so that we don't have to own it or change. |
| **Denial** | Excluding threatening or painful thoughts and feelings from awareness; refusing to accept the truth or reality of a fact or experience | • Unowned aspects of self will often be suppressed from awareness.<br>• la, la, la, la, la . . . |
| **Repression / Revision** | Simply forgetting bad and painful memories or revising those stories to remove the painful aspects | • The history of the conflict and of the relationship is often revised.<br>• Awareness of the conflict itself is repressed. |
| **Regression** | Reverting to a child-like emotional state | • We throw a tantrum like a small child. |
| **Displacement** | Discharging impulses by shifting from a threatening object to a "safer target" | • We attack someone else in the office (or the dog at home) instead of dealing with the person with whom we are angry. |
| **Rationalization (Justification)** | Manufacturing "good" reasons to explain away a bruised ego | • Reasons for the attack on others are often manufactured (blaming the victim). |

43 Table adapted from Gerald Corey, *Theory and Practice of Counseling and Psychotherapy*, 7th ed. (Belmont, CA: Brooks Cole, 2005), 59–60.

We all, at times, use various defense mechanisms to handle perceived ego threats. To some degree, this is normal. Sometimes,
however, we get stuck in one or more of these defenses. This
moves us further toward the emergence of conflict. Defense
mechanisms are the psychological strategies for defending
ourselves from the shame of not achieving or obtaining those
things we have deemed essential to our well-being. They often
work as part of a larger principle known as *scripting*.

## Life Scripting

We all have life scripts. They are deeply rooted in our past experiences, particularly early childhood, but also later in life. They
are essentially cognitive and emotional maps that become
triggered in interactions with others. When we are acting out
of our life script, we are not dealing with the present situation
but rather with unfinished business (vertical stress) from earlier
in life. Defense mechanisms are often driven by subconscious
life scripting connected to our families of origin. The story
we tell ourselves about ourselves is like a tape running in the
background of our current life situations. Psychologist Harry
Levinson connected the family and the workplace:

> All organizations recapitulate the basic family structure. . . . Our
> earliest experiences with our parents are repeated in our subse-
> quent relationships with authority. Early family life determines our
> assumptions of how power is distributed, and as we grow up we
> form groups on the same model. . . . If everyone knows what the
> rules are, things run smoothly. Since a business and a family share
> similar psychodynamics, you find the same sorts of problems in
> business—or any organizations—that you uncover in therapy.[44]

---

44 Harry Levinson quoted in Goleman, *Vital Lies Simple Truths: The Psychology of
Self-Deception* (New York: Simon & Schuster, 1985), 190–1.

When we experience a perceived ego threat, the script kicks in. We often do not realize in the moment that we are fighting someone who's not there, a ghost from our past.[45] Nonetheless, in workplace situations, this subconscious principle is in play. We begin to formulate defense mechanisms to protect ourselves from loss of personal esteem and begin to utilize these defenses as part of an attack against the perceived threat. Conflict begins to emerge.

Psychological defenses driven by insecurity or life scripting do not entirely explain the presence of conflict. It is common to explain away deeper culpability through this paradigm. Upon closer scrutiny, however, another principle emerges to clarify the root problem under the development of the near future attack.

## THE PROBLEM OF EVIL

There are psychological explanations for our conflict behavior that results from not receiving the object of our desire. However, there is an alternate or even parallel explanation: the potential for human evil.

What is your view of the following: genocide, ethnic cleansing, incest, rape, torture, murder, pedophilia? These are typically understood as evil actions, even by self-professed agnostics or atheists. What is your view of the following people: Adolf Hitler, Charles Manson, Pol Pot, Joseph Stalin, Osama bin Laden, Ted Bundy? Why did these people do what they did? Were they merely misunderstood? Did they suffer from insecurity or an inferiority complex? Or do you believe in the existence of human

---

45 James Framo's object relations therapy centers on these "ghosts" that are frequently the real opponents in marital conflict. Ghosts are most often significant attachment figures from earlier in life (parents, spouses, siblings, etc.).

evil? I'm not using evil in a religious sense, though for many it derives from religious beliefs and background. This present discussion of evil is not a religious argument. Evil is a recognizable human phenomenon for all of us.

Not all aggression (conflict) is based in ego defense mechanisms deriving from a lack of self-esteem or a wounded ego.

**Sometimes, the best explanation for the presence of conflict is the problem of human evil— a character problem.**

Think about the problem of bullying, a specific form of workplace and school yard conflict. The stereotype of the bully as a foolish oaf with a poor self-image has been shown to be, at best, half of the story. Is it true that people who attack others are always acting out of their own low self-image? Is narcissism a cover for insecurity? Or, as some have shown, is the problem of bullying more accurately understood as an overly positive sense of ego?

> People with low self-esteem tend to blame themselves when things go wrong. People with high self-esteem tend to blame external factors, such as other people, the situation, or various obstacles. . . . Thinking that all your problems and failures are your own fault is a style that fits low self-esteem. Thinking that nothing bad should ever reflect on you is an integral part of high self-esteem. . . . violent people tend to follow the high-self-esteem pattern.[46]

Many of the individuals listed earlier fit this description. Instead of suffering from inferiority complexes, they deemed themselves superior. It was that sense of superiority that gave them permission to pursue evil ends.

---

46 Roy Baumeister, *Evil: Inside Human Violence and Cruelty* (New York: Henry Holt, 1999), 153.

# THE ROOT OF WORKPLACE BULLYING: INFERIORITY OR SUPERIORITY?

In the 1980s, the American workplace began to be aware of sexual harassment. As an awareness of workplace sexual aggression advanced, the corporate world soon became aware of other forms of workplace aggression or bullying. More recently, our culture has become attuned to more subtle forms of mistreatment and disrespect, sometimes referred to as incivility.

Though the awareness of workplace bullying, in all its forms, has increased, the understanding of the nature and motivation underneath these behaviors has lagged behind. Many still subscribe to the concept that all bullies act from a deep sense of inferiority and low self-esteem. However, there is just as much evidence that bullying arises from high self-esteem as there is that it springs from the inverse. The origin of the problem of bullying is often threatened egotism: someone's ego being bruised by not getting what they deserve and using bullying as a bad coping method.

The Demand Model of conflict development postulates that conflict arises not from feelings or thoughts of inferiority but rather of superiority and entitlement, strands of narcissism that permeate our culture. It is interesting that in Judeo–Christian thought, the origin of evil does not spring from low self-esteem but from a luciferic problem of pride, envy, and a desire to be worshiped. Workplace bullying and aggression, the clearest forms of interpersonal conflict, seem to be similarly driven.

In his highly researched and seminal work on the problem of human evil, psychologist Philip Zimbardo defined his focus:

> [Human] evil consists in intentionally behaving in ways that harm, abuse, demean, dehumanize, or destroy innocent others—or using

one's authority and systemic power to encourage or permit others to do so on your behalf.[47]

Through the lens of defense mechanisms and scripting, aggressors are acting in less-than-fully intentional ways. One of the ways to distinguish evil from psychological explanations is this aspect of intentionality. Evil, it seems, is a choice we make. It involves being intentional.

Evil is related to the playing field problem. The field isn't level. Entropy causes things to move toward disharmony and chaos. And evil seems to be a part of that principle.

> Evil in human affairs is analogous to the process of entropy in the material universe. We call evil that which causes pain, suffering, disorder in the psyche or the community. . . . Entropy or evil is the default state, the condition to which the system returns unless work is done to prevent it. What prevents it is what we call "good" [*health or functionality*].[48]

If evil exists and is at least part of the problem if not the main portion, we are immediately confronted with a personal dilemma. Can we say of ourselves, that at some level, the conflicts we initiate are the result of our own intentional choices that derive from our lower nature?

## Not Out There, But In Here

Many of us tend to think of evil as a propensity belonging to others. It is a dispositional problem that *we* do not have. It is far too easy for us to condemn others as "evil" while not concur-

---

47 Philip Zimbardo, *The Lucifer Effect: Understanding How Good People Turn Evil* (New York: Random House, 2007), 5 (italics added).

48 Csikszentmihalyi, *Finding Flow*, 146 (italics added).

rently recognizing seeds of the same behaviors in ourselves. As
Roy Baumeister said, however,

> Understanding evil begins with the realization that we ourselves
> are capable of doing many of these things. . . . To understand evil,
> we must set aside the comfortable belief that we would never do
> anything wrong. Instead, we must begin to ask ourselves, what
> would it take for *me* to do such things? Assume that it would be
> possible.[49]

Evil is something of which we are all capable. Zimbardo's research confirms that given the right situation, the right catalysts,
many of us who otherwise would never dream of committing
acts labeled evil are more than willing to perpetrate the same.

This incorrect placement of the problem onto others through
projection allows us to pretend that evil isn't inside of us. Quinn
said,

> "Because the problem is out there, it is always others who need to
> change. Our first thought is to tell them to change. Our second is
> to force them."[50]

This is precisely how Scott Peck defined the nature of evil.
Working with clients from highly dysfunctional families, Peck
was able to catalog symptoms of these clients' families that
together made them "people of the lie." The fundamental lie is
found in their complete inability to see themselves as they are
and in their constant campaign of projecting the problems that
reside in themselves onto others around them.

> Strangely enough, evil people are often destructive because they
> are attempting to destroy evil. The problem is that they misplace

49 Baumeister, *Evil*, 5.

50 Quinn, *Deep Change*, 33.

the locus of evil. Instead of destroying others, they should be de-stroying the sickness within themselves.[51]

## The Blurring of Evil and Defenses

Evil itself, a form of self-deception, is a form of ego defense. The essence of evil is the inability to see ourselves as we are and a corresponding tendency to project those unwanted parts of self onto others who bear the brunt of our attack. We project, scapegoat, and do whatever is needed to keep the lie we tell ourselves alive, that the problem is not us. This makes us doubly people of the lie. We lie to ourselves and to others around us.

# DEVALUATION

When we encounter perceived opposition to our wants that have escalated to demands, we either begin to defend our ego with various strategies (defense mechanisms) or we simply disdain our opponent (evil). Either of these or both in concert move us toward the devaluation that always precedes the emer-gence of attack in conflict. Demand hardly ever moves straight into attack. It usually moves through defense mechanisms or human evil into devaluing our opponent. This usually less-than-fully conscious process happens in milliseconds.

All people are endued with certain inalienable rights as human beings. The founding fathers referred to these rights as en-dowed or given by divine proclamation. All people are entitled to being treated with dignity. This is not an earned right, nor is it able to be forfeited. Even criminals, in just societies, have certain rights that are inviolable. They have inherent worth and should

51 M. Scott Peck, *People of the Lie: The Hope for Healing Human Evil* (New York: Touchstone, 1983), 74.

be valued as such. These are the nobler principles involved in humanity.

Devaluing others contradicts this view of humanity. It is an essential psychological truth and a key to dissecting the true nature of conflict. If we allow ourselves to see our opponent as a human being, worthy of our respect and rightful treatment, most of us would be unable to carry out the attack. Knowledge of these inalienable aspects of our opponent must be suppressed before we can move forward. In order to proceed, we must devalue our opponent. Once devalued, our actions toward them seem less obscene. Devaluing our opponent is our way of tearing down or going around the wall.

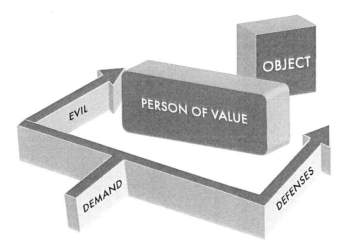

**Figure 6.** Getting around the wall.

A classic example of this principle can be found in the nature of prejudice and ethnic cleansing. Stereotypes of the targeted group are used to create a less-than-human caricature of the opponent. This is propaganda. The enemy is dehumanized, reduced in standing, and no longer viewed as our fellow man.

The Nazis' experimentation and misinformation suggested that non-Arians were an inferior less-than-human species. This philosophic devaluation opened the door for the atrocities of Auschwitz and other extermination camps.

## CONFLICT AS ATTACK

When a demand is processed through the dual filters of ego defenses and evil, it moves toward devaluing an opponent. Devalued and dehumanized opponents are then easily attacked. Conflict emerges into the light when these attacks are initiated. Prior to crossing this last remaining threshold, the conflict has remained a private, intrapersonal reality in the heart and mind of the individual. When the line is crossed, however, that which was intrapersonal now becomes interpersonal. That which was hidden now becomes visible. Interpersonal conflict proper, as evidenced by tangible attacks, has begun.

These attacks that characterize conflict are of two interrelated types that often work in concert with one another. This two-pronged strategy consists in the one–two punch of direct and indirect attacks.

## DIRECT ATTACK

A direct attack is, as it sounds, the initiation of some form of directly targeted aggression toward a perceived opponent. It is the implementation of specific assaults aimed at damaging the enemy in some way. These direct attacks, various expressions of workplace aggression and team conflict, come in predictable forms:

- Incivility. A way of passive–aggressively sending a message that an opponent doesn't matter. It is "the exchange of seemingly inconsequential inconsiderate words and deeds that violate conventional norms of workplace conduct."[52] Examples of incivility include interrupting a conversation, arriving late to meetings, being nonresponsive to questions, showing disrespect in front of others, and keeping people out of the loop.

- Constant, unfair, and unwarranted criticism or undermining.

- Harassment (sexual, psychological, physical, verbal).

- Bullying. This can be defined as follows:

  Bullying at work is repeated, health-harming mistreatment of a person by one or more workers that takes the form of verbal abuse; conduct or behaviors that are threatening, intimidating, or humiliating; sabotage that prevents work from getting done; or some combination of the three.[53]

- Gas-lighting and other crazy-making strategies. Gas-lighting is a specific and insidious form of emotional abuse that causes victims to begin to doubt themselves into thinking they are going crazy. The term originated from the 1944 Ingrid Bergman movie of the same name.[54]

- Diminishing job responsibilities, position, or authority.

- Wrongful termination.

## INDIRECT ATTACK

The American workplace has become much more sophisticated in recent years. Awareness of the nature of direct workplace ag-

---

52 Christine Pearson and Christine Porath, *The Cost of Bad Behavior: How Incivility Is Damaging Your Business and What to Do about It* (New York: Penguin Group, 2009), 12.

53 Gary Namie and Ruth Namie, *The Bully at Work: What You Can Do to Stop the Hurt and Reclaim Your Dignity on the Job* (Naperville, IL: Sourcebooks, 2009), 3.

54 If you suspect you're being "gas-lighted," read Robin Stern, *The Gaslight Effect: How to Spot and Survive the Hidden Manipulation Others Use to Control Your Life.*

gression and harassment has forced many conflicts to move toward indirect channels of expression. Indirect attacks consist in various means of seeking to destroy an opponent with plausible deniability. Here are some of the more common indirect attack strategies:

- Gossip and rumors are spread throughout the organization or the team as a way to discredit the target of the attack.

- Slander and misinformation differ from gossip in that they include false and misleading information used to discredit and defame the target.

- Avoidance and isolation seek to harm the victim even though the attacker can claim to have done nothing.

- "The Mental Health Trap" is a favorite form of indirect bullying and discrediting the victim.

The target is often unaware of many of these indirect attacks. They can feel the aftereffects but are left with only speculation as to what was said to whom within the organization. This one–two punch is normally quite devastating to the target of the aggression.

# THE MENTAL HEALTH TRAP

Tim Field, in his work *Bully in Sight*, aptly described a form of indirect attack known as the mental health trap. Many aggressors employ the tactic of ongoing bullying, a form of direct attack. As an ongoing direct attack in various forms is carried out, the target often begins to show signs of psychological weakening. This psychiatric injury, caused externally by the hostile work environment, is portrayed to onlookers as the victim's mental illness. The bully, often a person in authority over the victim, offers the suffering employee mental health assistance. They appear to be compassionate in offering help and simultaneously trap their victims as follows:

> If the person consents (and their need is dire), they are admitting they have a "mental health problem." If they decline, the battering continues, with the bully pointing out that the victim is resisting accepting professional help.[55]

This tactic puts the victim in a real catch-22 situation. In reality, there is a significant difference between the external origin of psychological symptoms (PTSD) resulting from prolonged bullying and internal origins of depressive symptoms due to victim illness. Depression caused externally is quite different than depression that arises from the patient.

# RESULTANT DAMAGE

The end result of conflict in the form of direct and indirect attacks is damage done to one or both parties involved. This is the culmination of the Demand Model that has been described. Where there is no damage, there is no conflict proper. This is the very damage we seek to prevent. Once it has occurred, we

---

55 Tim Field, *Bully in Sight: How to Predict, Resist, Challenge, and Combat Workplace Bullying* (Oxfordshire, UK: Success Unlimited, 1996), 135.

find ourselves in need of reparative strategies. When the conflict fully emerges in the form of substantive, relational, and personal damages, most often intervention strategies will be needed to restore the team and the individuals who have suffered loss.

## Substantive (Material) Damage

Conflicts often cause damage that can be quantified. This can be in the form of assets or financial damage but also in the form of personal reputation, business reputation in the community, and so forth. These damages can often be repaired through financial or other means (restitution). They can be the most costly but, in a sense, the most readily repairable.

## Relational Damage

Relationships are another story. Often, relationships that existed prior to the conflict and the ensuing damage are no longer recoverable. When they are, these can become some of the deepest human relationships. Two people who have experienced significant conflict and are able to do the hard work of restoration form a unique bond. This damage is always much harder to quantify and involves soft interpersonal aspects like honesty, trust, and vulnerability.

## Personal Damage

Personal damage is the damage done to the person who is the target of conflict. Most often, this is the invisible injury to the inner life and well-being of the person who has endured psychological assaults. Sense of self is often directly affected in the midst of powerful conflict dynamics. We are beginning to understand the effects of war on our veterans as they come home with either PTSD or traumatic brain injuries or both. In the United States, we lag behind the rest of the world in understanding similar damage that results from noncombat, psychological warfare in the workplace.

## THE DEMAND MODEL OF CONFLICT DEVELOPMENT

We have been exploring conflict, developing from its contributors, emerging from within an aggressor, and escalating into an interpersonal attack against an opponent. This is a fifth model of conflict, the Demand Model. In this model, conflict proper emerges as the end result of the energy from unmet demands moving through ego defenses or evil that culminates in the devaluation of our opponent, creating the rationale for our attack. When we attack, we cause damage. Figure 7 shows the progression.

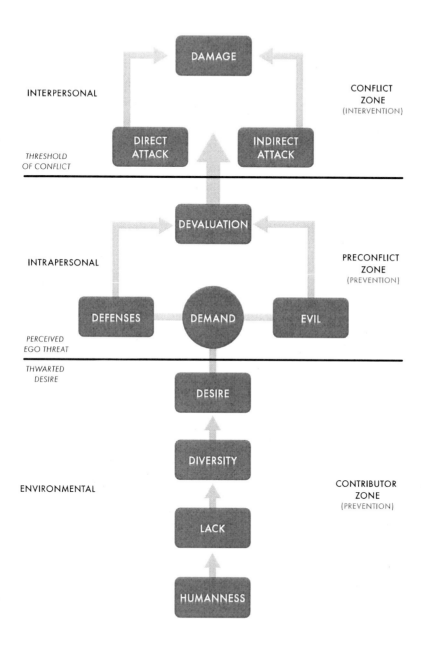

**Figure 7.** The Demand Model of conflict development.

The Demand Model of conflict helps explain the manner in which a conflict emerges from the environment, growing intrapersonally until it becomes interpersonal. As my friend and colleague Randy Lisk has put it, "All models are wrong; some are useful."[56] This imperfect model of conflict, as all models are, helps explain the development of a phenomenon many of us may not have spent significant effort trying to understand.

Because of our aversion to painful topics like conflict, we tend not to deeply analyze them. We need to be careful that our lack of understanding of topics like this doesn't make us susceptible to endlessly repeating the same cycle and never adequately stopping to reflect on the past. As Edmund Burke said, "Those who don't understand history are destined to repeat it." The hope in offering this model for explaining conflict in the midst of an increasingly narcissistic society is that it will provide us the opportunity to prevent it.

# WORKING DEFINITION

Gathering all that we have said thus far, we can attempt to construct a working definition of interpersonal conflict:

> *The committal of direct or indirect attacks, resulting in substantive, relational, or personal damage against those who have been devalued. They have been devalued through the use of defense mechanisms and/or according to evil intent as a result of a perceived hindrance or denial of a rightful demand.*

Problem solutions and problem definitions are interrelated. Our understanding of the nature of the problem guides our approach to both prevention and resolution. Before we discuss these two critical topics, one more aspect of conflict situations needs to be addressed: conflict occurs interpersonally within systems.

---

56 Randy Lisk, *Bumper Sticker Leadership: One-Liner Wisdom on Life and Business* (Boise, ID: Aloha Publishing, 2012), 22.

# 4

# SYSTEMS AND CONFLICT

Thus far, we've examined conflict primarily through the lens of an individual model or intrapersonally. Conflict, in the Demand Model, emerges as the result of unmet requirements on the part of one person, the aggressor. Though antagonists most often involve others in their attack against the person perceived to be a threat, the push toward conflict is largely driven from within the individual's inner life. In this chapter, we want to expand our thinking to include the group dynamics involved in the development and maintenance of conflict in a team or organization.

## SYSTEMS THEORY APPLIED TO ORGANIZATIONS

Beginning in the 1920s, men like Ludwig von Bertalanffy, Alfred North Whitehead, and Paul Weiss began to articulate concepts that have come to be known as systems theory. The world at that time was narrowly focused on specialization and the particularity of each separate discipline. Systems theory began to bring the focus back onto the whole, seeing the system in its entirety as a composite, rather than considering each part separately. From that time to the present, systemic thinking has become a key to understanding various disciplines, in particular family systems and other similar interpersonal systems, such as the workplace group or organization.

Following the industrial revolution, the emerging field of management was highly influenced by Frederick W. Taylor. Taylor's model was called "scientific management" and viewed people as "resources." These human resources were motivated by reward (money) linked to personal output in a classical carrot-and-stick fashion. In the 1920s, in reaction to the dehumanizing of Taylorism, the Human Relations School of Management emerged, putting emphasis back onto the laborers as "people." Workplace conditions and the overall environment began to be emphasized as humane motivations in the workplace. In the 1940s, Abraham Maslow's hierarchy of needs in the field of psychology became popular, and for the next few decades, various individuals introduced concepts derived from it into the American workplace. Companies began to think of success as moving as many employees as possible to higher levels of Maslow's pyramid, which culminated in self-actualization.

Picking up on the General Systems Theory of van Bertalanffy, the psychological community consisting of now infamous leaders, such as Jay Haley (1923–2007), Gregory Bateson (1904–1980), Virginia Satir (1916–1988), Salvador Minuchin (1921–), and Murray Bowen (1913–1990), began to introduce to the therapeutic world several versions of family systems theory and therapy. Concurrent with this development of systems theory in family counseling and business management in the United States, a statistician by the name of W. Edwards Deming (1900–1993) worked with industry in Japan to increase manufacturing efficiency and quality. His findings in Japan and the United States seemed to confirm his suspicion that most problems in the workplace are systemic. *The recurring problems weren't about bad people, but rather about bad systems of management.*

Systems thinking is now a permanent part of our understanding of human relationships and groups. In every environment, family, workplace, social group, or organization of any kind, systems theory and thinking are critical aspects of our explanation of the dynamics of conflict.

## THE TEAM AS A SYSTEM

A system is a group of individuals that functions as a whole, a team. The system is greater than any individual member and has a life of its own that is larger and more powerful than any of the individuals who comprise it. The work team is a system, often a subsystem of a larger system known as the organization. Members of the team are interconnected at the core of who they are as human beings.

## THE SOCIAL INTELLIGENCE CONNECTION

Human beings are inherently relational creatures. We are built for connection with one another and cannot avoid our interconnectedness. Though we have suspected this anecdotally throughout the history of our species, recent scientific research confirms the empirical basis behind our suspicions. The burgeoning field known as social intelligence studies this phenomenon. Research has confirmed the presence of neurological structures in our brains that render us intrinsically connected, whether we like it or not. Many structures within our brains make this interconnection a certainty. Here are just a few:

- "**Mirror neurons** reflect back an action we observe in someone else, making us mimic that action or have the impulse to do so."[57]

---

57 Daniel Goleman and Daniel Stern, *Social Intelligence: The New Science of Human Relationships* (New York: Bantam Dell, 2006), 41.

- **Oscillators** are "neural systems that act like clocks, reset-ting over and over their rate of firing to coordinate with an incoming signal."[58]

- **Attachment patterns**, visible with functional MRIs, show neural pathways that have resulted from childhood and subsequent development.

- **Spindle cells**, super rapid connectors of the social brain (family-of-origin impacted), bond the high and low roads (our rational and emotion brain pathways).[59]

Science now confirms that in light of what we understand about our brains, we can no longer remain ignorant about this prin-ciple of social intelligence. As Goleman and Stern pointed out,

> We can no longer . . . "see our minds as so independent, separated, and isolated," but instead we must view them as "permeable," con-tinually interacting as though *joined by an invisible link*.[60]

Social intelligence confirms the reality of our systemic connec-tion to one another. Our connection is at many levels. First and foremost, we are connected emotionally.

## EMOTIONAL CONTAGION

Have you ever found yourself yawning after witnessing a co-worker doing the same? Do you similarly find yourself impacted by the emotions around you in the workplace? When a team member is upset, do you and others on the team feel it? Of course you do. This is the manner in which emotional contagion spreads through the team, according to the power of social in-

---

58 Ibid., 34.

59 Ibid., 158.

60 Ibid., 43 (italics added).

telligence. We've all experienced it; now we have scientific data to explain its existence.

Emotional contagion, for good or ill, spreads across the team through this reality of social intelligence. For this reason, it is incumbent on leaders at every level to understand this dynamic and to seek to lead their respective teams by example. Izzy Justice, the cocreator of the TTI emotional intelligence survey, described this responsibility of leadership:

> The leaders at an organization set the tone and culture for interpersonal interaction. The leaders' EQ affects their team's emotions and actions. Such emotional contagion travels down the chain in an organization, ultimately affecting your customer's emotions and buying behaviors to affect your bottom line.[61]

As Izzy described this process, he rightfully reminded us that the contagion doesn't stop at the boundary of our team but continues to affect others, including our customers and clients.

Our teams, then, are a system of interconnected individuals who mutually influence each other in various ways, most notably in levels of emotional intelligence, through the built-in functions of our brains that we call social intelligence. This underlines the importance of developing emotional intelligence throughout the organization within each member of the team. EQ matters.[62]

## TEAM SYSTEMS DYNAMICS

Compare office team dynamics and family groups.[63] This is not only easy to do but is actually helpful in understanding team

---

61 Izzy Justice, *EQmentor Delivers Results* (Cornelius, NC: EQmentor Inc., 2011), 3.

62 See appendix C: Emotional Intelligence.

63 If the business is a family business, the two are often the same or have significant overlap.

conflict. From a family systems perspective, the problem (in the marriage and family therapist's office) is not any one member of the family but the family itself. Each member of the family plays a role that is part of the system. Good family therapists understand this and work with the family *system* as the *client*, helping them to understand that the identified patient is not the problem. Moving the client (the family) away from placing blame on one individual is part of good family therapy. Each person in the family and the family as a whole make contributions to the ongoing dynamics of the family (for better and for worse).

**The problem is the system.**

## GREATER THAN THE SUM OF THE PARTS

The team is greater than the sum of the individuals who comprise it. In systems thinking, one plus one doesn't only equal two. There is an additional piece of the equation created in the midst of the synergy. For systems, the total is almost always greater than the sum of the individual contributions. This is particularly true as it pertains to power in the system. The system as a whole has far greater power than the sum total of each of the persons within it. This explains, in part, why one individual often rightly feels powerless to change an unhealthy system.

## HOMEOSTASIS, RESISTANCE TO CHANGE

Homeostasis is the normal position of the system, the status quo. Systems theory maintains that all systems will ultimately seek a return to homeostasis, life as usual (not necessarily life as healthy). The workplace team is no exception. Change agents from within or from outside of the system will almost invariably encounter resistance from group members and the system as a whole. Sometimes these change agents are punished by the system for attempting to rock the boat. Conflict results.

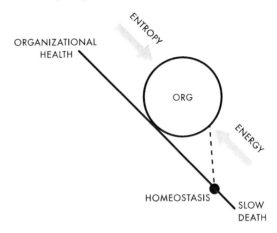

**Figure 8.** Homeostasis as an anchor preventing progress.

As you can see illustrated, homeostasis is like an anchor that hinders movement in either direction. Our greatest concern is the effect it has on potential growth toward health as we seek to move the organization uphill.

## PROJECTION OF SYMPTOMS

In dysfunctional family systems, there is most often an identified patient. This person's role in the system is to be the bearer of the family's pain, agreeing to be the one who carries the bulk of the family's symptoms. This is most often the patient that the family refers for counseling. Good therapists, however, are highly attuned to this frequent family ploy. They are able to see clearly the way the family seeks to project its symptoms onto the identified patient.

As it is in dysfunctional families, so it often is in the workplace. Teams will project symptoms onto a scapegoat that the team or a leader has unconsciously chosen to be the bearer of the system's dysfunction. When we ask a teammate, "What's wrong with so-and-so?" in the context of a systemic problem, we may be drifting toward this phenomenon. The scapegoat is often named as the "real problem." Scott Peck described this systemic dysfunction:

> A predominant characteristic, however, of the behavior of those I call evil is *scapegoating*. Because in their hearts they consider themselves above reproach, they must lash out at anyone who does reproach them. They sacrifice others to preserve their self-image of perfection. . . . Scapegoating works through a mechanism psychiatrists call projection. Since the evil, deep down, feel themselves to be faultless, it is inevitable that when they are in conflict with the world, they will invariably perceive the conflict as the world's fault. Since they must deny their own badness, they must perceive others as bad. They project their own evil onto the world.[64]

The team, as a system, projects its problems onto an identified patient whose job becomes to carry the systemic-driven pain away. This person is often the target of individual or group aggression in the form of various sorts of conflict behavior. Sometimes this person is terminated as a way to "solve the problem" and "move forward."

People who are scapegoated are usually not the problem. Ironically, scapegoats are usually quite capable and responsible people. Their goodness is used against them by the system. Namie and Namie described some of the top reasons individuals are bullied:

> [*They possess*] self-confidence . . . superior competence or technical skill. . . . [*They are the*] "go-to" employee trusted by everyone else to know the answers to difficult questions. . . . [*They have good*] social skills. . . . [*They report*] being liked, [*having a*] positive attitude. [*They are*] ethical, honest [*people*]. . . . Targets don't have an integrity problem.[65]

---

64 Peck, *People of the Lie*, 73–74 (italics added).
65 Namie and Namie, *The Bully at Work*, 56–59 (italics added).

The identified patient isn't the problem. The system can't look at the real problem, so it looks for an alternative explanation. The selection of the identified patient is just another symptom of the sickness in the system.

## GROUPTHINK

One last system dynamic is worthy of discussion when we think about working groups and conflict development. It is the phenomenon known as groupthink. Groupthink is an unhealthy communication pattern that develops in an unhealthy system. In this mode, the group shares a collective mind. The clear thinking of each individual is sacrificed for the common thought of the group. What *I* think is no longer relevant; it has given sway to what *we* think. This phenomenon is common among all groups experiencing conflict, specifically with work teams. Groupthink is reinforced by propaganda, repeated messages aimed at the devaluation of the common enemy.

Groupthink is the force underneath group conflict, sometimes referred to as mobbing. In mobbing, the group uses its power against an individual target of aggression. One of the telltale signs of the presence of groupthink and mobbing is the overuse of the word "we" in the description of the team's perception of the problem. What *I* think gives way to what *we* think.

## SYSTEM AS PROBLEM

Deming, the famous originator of Total Quality Management, famously believed that 85 percent of the recurring problems in an organization is systemic, management problems, whereas only 15 percent of recurring problems can be attributed to the employees themselves. This is the Deming 85/15 rule, a systemic explanation for the presence of problems and conflict in the workplace.

After years of looking at systemic conflict through the lens of his research done at Stanford and Abu Ghraib, Philip Zimbardo offered a similar thought:

> Most of us have a tendency both to overestimate the importance of dispositional [*what we are calling character*] qualities and to underestimate the importance of situational qualities [*what we are calling contributors or systemic aspects*] when trying to understand the causes of other people's [*bad*] behavior. . . . Situational conditions are created and shaped by higher order factors—systems of power. Systems, not just dispositions and situations, must be taken into account in order to understand complex behavior patterns.[66]

Robert Quinn also pointed to the systemic nature of problems:

> Every organization has a group of systems. . . . In an environment of constant change, each of these systems . . . tends to wear down. Alignment within and between systems is lost. We find ourselves working harder than ever, yet we benefit less and less from our efforts. As tension mounts, we look for someone to blame. *The real problem, however, is embedded in the underlying organizational systems* that have shifted out of alignment—with each other and sometimes with the external environment.[67]

In the analysis of these three experts and many others, the system itself, at a fundamental level, is the problem. Sometimes, we search in vain for personally responsible individuals who are deficient in terms of their disposition, and we would do better to understand the presence of evil or conflict in light of the power systems in play. In other words, the evil is sometimes systemic.

### Some systems are dysfunctional at the core.

Dysfunctional systems actually encourage or promote aggression between team members. The only way to personally survive these toxic systems is to extricate oneself from them entirely. These uncoachable systems have systemic problems that

---

66 Zimbardo, *Lucifer Effect*, 8–10 (italics added).

67 Quinn, *Deep Change*, 60 (italics added).

condone and encourage the intrapersonal and interpersonal development and maintenance of conflict in the organizational culture.[68]

## SYSTEMIC CONTRIBUTIONS TO CONFLICT

Often, however, it is the case that both systemic and individual contributions to conflict exist concurrently. When conflict is driven through individual demands, the system that surrounds the team often contributes indirectly to the conflict situation. This indirect contribution normally comes in three predictable forms.

## SILENTLY CONDONING CONFLICT (NEUTRALITY)

Sadly, in many organizations, the response to conflict or its precursors is to do nothing. This is a form of abdication on the part of the leadership; individuals who could exert a shaping influence on the culture of the tribe do nothing. Such is the case with workplace bullying and aggression, one of the most overt expressions of workplace conflict. In such cases, the perpetrator escalates toward the eventual attack. The real cause and the corresponding ultimate blame for the presence of conflict can be found in the bully. However, when the system the bully operates in does nothing to stop the ongoing onslaught of aggression, it becomes culpable in a conspiratorial manner. Who is ultimately to blame for the continued allowance of bullying in the American workplace? Namie and Namie unequivocally asserted that it is the employers who are primarily to blame:

> Bullying is the scourge of the contemporary workplace, but it is too easily ignored by the people who could eradicate it if they were motivated, the residents of the C-suites—executives, administrators,

---

68 These are normally tribal stage 1 or 2 cultures according to the Logan et al. model introduced in chapter 7.

and owners. . . . All international laws firmly fix *responsibility for pre-vention and correction on employers.* The United States is dead last.[69]

One of the ways the system indirectly contributes to the ongo-ing conflict is through abdication of its authority. Its silence con-dones the attack.

> **The system could stop it if it took its role in conflict**
> **prevention seriously, but it chooses not to**
> **get its hands dirty.**

## COVERING UP (UNHEALTHY SANCTUARY)

Sanctuary is a medieval term for the protection provided by the church to people wrongfully charged with offenses. The walls of the cathedral provided temporary protection from the pos-sibility of overzealous justice. The core assumption, importantly, is that of innocence on the part of the person being sheltered. Sometimes companies and organizations provide unhealthy sanctuary to people who are far from innocent. We've seen many recent examples of this principle in corporate America.

The system indirectly contributes to the maintenance of con-flict through a more active cover-up of the growing evidence of the problem. The organization goes into damage control mode, circles the wagons, and begins to do whatever it feels is neces-sary to maintain the illusion that all is well. "No conflict here." The system always has more power than the individual (unless a higher authority such as the state becomes the advocate for the individual). The outcome is predictable. The system that refuses to acknowledge its internal problems will prevail over the latest victim and continue to live in a repetitive cycle of dysfunction.

---

69 Namie and Namie, *The Bully at Work*, xiv–xv (italics added).

# THE BUSH DOCTRINE

Shortly after the events of September 11, 2001, President George W. Bush began to articulate what has been dubbed the Bush Doctrine. Since that time, the concept has been broadened to include any number of foreign policy concepts, including the right to preemptive strikes at the whim of the American leader. The concept has fallen victim to the unpopularity of the former president connected to it. However, the basic idea that President Bush originally articulated is worthy of remembrance. Whatever your political stance, whether a lover or hater of Bush, you may be able to see some validity in the doctrine's core idea as it was originally stated.

President Bush, in the aftermath of the worst tragedy on American soil since Pearl Harbor, articulated his belief that the nations that had harbored and given sanctuary to the terrorists who plotted and carried out the atrocities of 9-11, should and would be held liable for the actions of those they had harbored. It wasn't just the terrorists, but those who had supported them, who had allowed them to do what they did, that he considered liable. He famously informed the American public that we would hold the terrorists and those who had supported them accountable for our national pain.

Many organizations, by doing nothing, allow internal "terrorists" of another sort to survive and threaten the overall health and well-being of employees within their organization. These do-nothing companies are like the nations threatened by the Bush Doctrine. By providing unhealthy sanctuary, they allow bullies at all levels to continue and thereby contribute to the creation of an unsafe work environment for everyone in their path.

## WILLFUL BLINDNESS

Willful blindness is a legal term that refers to someone's culpability when what they could and should have seen is willfully repressed from awareness. This kind of blindness takes place at all levels of teams and throughout the system.

In her research in the United States and abroad, Margaret Heffernan found a constant within organizations.[70] In 85 percent of organizations, the organization admitted there were ongoing issues that people were afraid to raise (and therefore doing nothing about them by exercising willful blindness). Why were they afraid? She found three dominant reasons:

1. They feared retaliation.

2. They believed that seeing or pointing out the problems was futile, that nothing would change anyway.

3. They didn't want to be known as a whistle-blower, because they carried a belief that informed them, "You know what happens to them."

Surprisingly, Heffernan found that the common thinking underlying the willfully blind about the nature of a whistle-blower was erroneous. Instead of whistle-blowers actually being "crazy," Heffernan found that most were very loyal, conservative, highly dedicated people who chose to do what they did out of a deep care for the health of the organization they served. Second, she found that instead of them being "crushed," they all shared a recurrent quality that she best identified as pride. Most whistle-blowers when asked if they would do it again in light of the cost that was exacted will reply "yes."

---

70 Information taken from Margaret Heffernan's TED Talk, "Willful Blindness," March 2013, accessed October 21, 2013, http://www.ted.com/talks/margaret_heffernan _the_dangers_of_willful_blindness.html.

Willful blindness takes place in leadership and among the ranks. It can happen at all levels of the organization or the team and is a systemic contributor to the ongoing problem of conflict.

## SYSTEMIC SOLUTIONS

The same system that has power to maintain the status quo has the power, if enough of the members are on board, to become part of the solution to conflict. Corporate cultures can be created, beginning with the leadership, that refuse to respond in any of the ways mentioned above. These cultural values of zero tolerance, no cover-up, and a rejection of willful blindness are essential for teams that want to move toward health and functionality. Healthy teams and organizations educate themselves in the area of conflict prevention and resolution. They become victim-aware and are no longer so readily duped by the repeat offenders who run over people to obtain their desires.

Conflict-friendly cultures unfortunately are legal, at least in the United States. Cultures that tolerate workplace conflict and continue to remain in denial or to actively cover for the perpetrators have systemic problems. These organizations are not the focus of this book. This book promotes a culture where conflict is not tolerated, not ignored, not denied, but actively and mutually worked through and successfully avoided through the active cultivation of healthy relationships. The courts aren't going to force us to be conflict-aware. It is a choice that we need to make on our own as a healthy team.

# 5

# CONFLICT PREVENTION

An ounce of prevention is worth a pound of cure. An apple a day keeps the doctor away. The best defense is a good offense. All of these truisms contain a similar idea. In the arena of conflict, the best prevention is found in the positive development of organizational health. Healthy relationships and increased levels of team development serve as protections against the development of conflict. In other words, team building is conflict prevention. The two are opposite sides of the same coin.

Team building is an ongoing process of strengthening relationships. Building teams is sometimes viewed with the same enthusiasm as joining a gym. The day we sign up (usually shortly after January 1), we have the best of intentions to develop new and healthier exercise habits. Our enthusiasm, however, soon wanes. Exercise is built on the quality of discipline. So it is with team building. Team building over the long haul requires the exercise of intentional and intense discipline. If team building (the positive side of the equation) loses momentum, conflict prevention is even harder to maintain. Peter Randall explained this mind-set:

> Conflict within the workplace is often thought to be an inevitable consequence of the "strange brew" of people and environments

[*diversity*] which, together, provide the social milieu of the workplace. This understanding often becomes a reassurance that although conflict is not pleasant, at least it is not unnatural [*human*] and not something that need be taken too seriously. Handy (1993) reminds us, however, that *to ignore conflict simply because its causes may seem trivial is to allow it to take hold within the organization and give it the opportunity to perpetuate itself.* Conflict may be natural, or at least it may be an inevitable ingredient of the human condition, but so is ill health, and society does a great deal to prevent or alleviate that amongst its members. So too should organizations seek to alleviate and prevent conflict.[71]

Active and ongoing conflict prevention is a must for teams and organizations that wish to achieve superior results and a good report regarding overall organizational health.

## WHY DOING NOTHING WON'T WORK

As Randall pointed out, many organizations and teams fail to recognize the potential for conflict development and fail to do anything to prevent it. If entropy is real, things will not spontaneously improve on their own. In fact, doing nothing ensures that things will eventually deteriorate. Failing to maintain relationships will ultimately result in relational deterioration in the form of conflict.

Doing nothing is doing something. Though we would like to think that the option of doing nothing is nonconsequential, this belief is delusional. Choosing "none of the above" is a choice nonetheless. Choosing "I'll deal with this later" is also a choice. The rock band Rush had it right, "if you choose not to decide, you still have made a choice."

---

71 Peter Randall, *Adult Bullying: Perpetrators and Victims* (New York: Brunner-Routledge, 2003), 131 (italics added).

## AN ACTIVE STRATEGY

The Demand Model of conflict suggests that the development of conflict follows a predictable path. To the extent that the model is accurate as a predictor, we shouldn't be surprised or blindsided by the predictable steps toward the emergence of workplace conflict. At every point along that progression, however, we are afforded an opportunity to prevent the inevitable. So, we typically have multiple chances at escalating levels in the contributor zone to stop the development in its tracks. If we miss it early and fail to act, there are normally additional opportunities to nip it in the proverbial bud, before it is allowed to fully bloom.

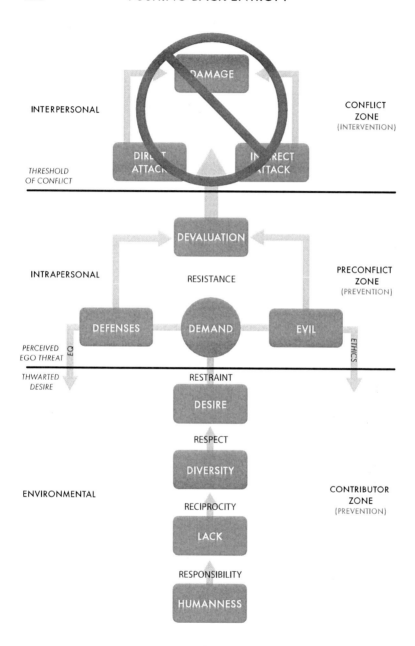

**Figure 9.** The Demand Model of conflict prevention.

If we overlay the Demand Model of conflict with preventative measures at each critical juncture, we begin to discern a model for conflict prevention. This diagram portrays the Demand Model of conflict prevention. Consider the following antidotes for the stepping stones toward conflict. We begin with personal responsibility, a trait of human beings who resist the temptation to excuse their bad behavior as "only human."

## RESPONSIBILITY, NOT HUMANNESS AS AN EXCUSE

We all struggle with similar things. This is the human condition. The appeal to our humanity, our finiteness, our imperfection and frailty, is not a valid excuse for our overt actions of aggression. It is so frequently cited as a blanket excuse, however, that we sometimes begin to believe our own rhetoric. We have been systematically conditioned to validate the concept of "not being able to help ourselves." Responsibility is the antidote to the excuse of humanness.

**We may all be human, but being fully human includes a healthy dose of personal and group responsibility.**

We are living in what many cultural experts refer to as a narcissistic age. This is the age of the *me* generation, the age of entitlement. Rights are far more popular than responsibilities (just google it). We enjoy hearing about our inalienable rights, inherent privileges, and basic entitlements. Responsibilities, not as much. Rights and responsibilities, however, always go together. The one who is given more in the form of the advantages of rights and privileges holds a greater level of personal responsibility. As Winston Churchill said, "The price of greatness is responsibility."[72] The need to underline this obvious aspect of

---

72 Winston Churchill, speech at Harvard University, 1943.

basic human character development is indicative of the age in which we find ourselves.

## RECIPROCITY, NOT IGNORING LACK

Lack, though not a valid excuse for the development of conflict, is a reality. Various types of scarcity exist, from being in want of the basic necessities of life (food, clothing, shelter) to the just as important needs of being loved, accepted, valued, and so on. When our needs are not met, when we are truly in want, the potential for conflict exists. Though we perceive ourselves as a never-enough society, in reality we are a nation of abundance. What we may need to relearn is the joy that comes from sharing with others who are less fortunate.

The principle of reciprocity is the antidote to the potential problem of lack and scarcity. Stated simply, this is the golden rule of doing unto others as we would have them do unto us. This is the higher human ideal of sharing with and caring for others, the altruistic principle. We are often able to meet the lack we identify in another's life. As each of us looks out not only for self, but for the best interest of others around us (team members, coworkers), we reduce this potential catalyst for future conflict development. It could be as simple as providing the gift of friendship or relationship to a coworker who is lonely. Reducing lack is often within our ability. When we do, we take fuel away from the fire of potential future conflict.

## RESPECT, NOT INTOLERANCE OF DIVERSITY

It's hard not to think of Aretha's famous song. More than simply spelling it out, respect is needed in healthy teams to counter the potential problem of diversity. Diversity itself is not the problem. Our inability to fully and wholeheartedly embrace it is. This principle was referred to by Howard Garder as the development of the "respectful mind." He wrote,

> The respectful mind notes and welcomes differences between human individuals and human groups, tries to understand these "others," and seeks to work effectively with them.[73]

What, then, does the cultivation of this kind of respect, a trait that will serve as a strong protection against conflicts on the team, look like? Chapter 1 outlined a substantial number of differences that exist between us as teammates.

**The simple and overriding answer to deepening mutual respect is character development.**

Oftentimes, specific areas of difference may need to be understood at a deeper level for this diversity to be viewed through new eyes. In our work with teams, this often consists of specific trainings in several key areas of focus:

## Diversity Training

There has been some progress made toward a healthy embrace of diversity in the American workplace, but there remains more room for progress. Unfortunately, issues such as ageism, racism, and sexism still exist and are a scourge on the organizational culture. These issues run deeply, have a long history, and are perpetuated through ongoing ignorance and an unhealthy form of groupthink.

Diversity can be taught. Group values and a shared culture can be developed and clearly articulated in the tribal language of

---

73 Howard Gardner, *Five Minds for the Future* (Boston: Harvard Business Press, 2008), 3.

the organization. As in other areas, this team quality begins at the top. Tribal leaders set the tone. As they actively value diversity, they exemplify the organizational values for others to follow.

## Behavioral Styles Training

The value that comes from integrating DISC language into the culture is enormous. As team members are better able to use the language of DISC to describe themselves and their teammates, new doors of mutual valuing open up. Understanding behavioral styles creates far better communication, reducing conflict that is driven by behavioral differences.[74]

## Motivators Training

Understanding differing passions and drives helps teammates learn to work better together for common goals. We have a natural tendency to overvalue what we value and to undervalue what others value. Training the team to understand motivator differences is a means of opening their eyes to the different passions that underlie the actions of those around them. They learn to understand instead of judge.

## Emotional Intelligence Training

Research continues to validate the importance of emotional intelligence to ever-increasing levels of team cohesion and performance. (EQ as a science is described in appendix C.) Teams that focus on increasing emotional intelligence are exponentially reducing the prevalence and probability of conflict.

---

74 If you haven't already, read appendix A: Behaviors. In our work with organizations, we spend a lot of time and focus on helping teams see themselves and others through the new lens of DISC as both a prevention of conflict and a critical team-building activity.

## Extroversion / Introversion / Ambiversion Training

Related to DISC (behavioral styles), this personality aspect continues to be a critical area of better understanding self and others. We live in an extrovert-biased culture. Extroverts and introverts can benefit from seeing this reality and learning the critical nature of creating balance on the team between these two fundamentally different ways of experiencing the world around us.

## TWO DIFFERENT NEURAL PATHWAYS

The difference between introversion and extroversion is neural. We process information differently in our brains.[75]

**Table 3.** Different Neural Pathways

| The Introverted Acetylcholine Pathway | The Extroverted Dopamine Pathway |
| --- | --- |
| **Reticular Activating System** More sensitive to outside stimulation | **Reticular Activating System** Less reactive than introverts, takes more stimulation to arouse |
| **Hypothalamus** Triggers the parasympathetic nervous system to conserve energy, lowering heart rate and blood pressure | **Hypothalamus** Triggers the sympathetic nervous system, activating fight-or-flight responses, increasing heart rate and blood pressure |
| **Anterior Thalamus** Acts as a relay station sending signals to the anterior cingulated gyrus and frontal lobe (longer path) | **Posterior Thalamus** Sends signals to the visual cortex and sensory association areas (shorter path) |

75 The table is adapted from Kyle Rohane, "Gray Matters: The Brains behind Our Personalities," *Leadership Journal* (2013): accessed October 21, 2013, http://www .outofur.com/archives/2013/06/gray _matters.html.

| The Introverted Acetylcholine Pathway | The Extroverted Dopamine Pathway |
|---|---|
| **Broca's Area**<br>Helps produce articulate speech through inner dialogue or self-talk | **Amygdala**<br>Responds positively to pleasant things (affirmation, positive feedback) |
| **Frontal Lobe**<br>The seat of cognitive function—aids in memory retrieval and planning, preparing for the future and learning from the past | **Temporal and Motor Area**<br>Connects movement to short-term memory to take in information, process it, and react quickly |
| **Hippocamus**<br>Tags experiences as "personal" | |
| **Amygdala**<br>Stores memories of painful and uncomfortable experiences as fear and anxiety | |

Introversion and extroversion are two extremes of a continuum. The midpoint between the two is referred to as ambiversion. As you can see illustrated, the neural pathway for the strong introvert is much longer than for the strong extrovert, which explains why the experience of each is so radically different.

## Character Development Training

If character can be viewed as the combination of EQ and ethics, additional training in the area of ethics will further reinforce the foundation of a healthy team and serve as preventative to the escalation of conflict above the threshold. Only a century ago, the vast majority of the literature regarding leadership development was character based. We may begin to see the shortcomings of our shift to a culture of personality and return to a culture of character.

Respect for others and wholehearted embrace of the beauty that comes from our diversity go a long way toward not only preventing conflict but creating a positive environment of safety and trust. Bellman and Ryan put it this way:

> Respect for differences makes it easier for members to bring their true selves to the group. People feel appreciated for who they are; they know that acceptance in the group does not require them to pretend to be someone else.... These dynamics promote a sense of safety and trust.... In this way, respect, safety—and the trust that follows—allow for full engagement.[76]

Respecting and accepting others as they are become keys to building healthy teams and preventing conflict. Accepting or embracing the differences doesn't mean that we don't see them or that we lose the healthy differences of opinion as diverse and unique individuals. It simply means that we think differently about those differences.

> Embracing differences is not about resolving conflicts or winning a debate; it is about welcoming and holding differences in a nurturing way, so that they can be seen, understood, and used as a resource to achieve a group's Purpose and Impact.... Without embracing differences, collaboration and innovation are impossible.[77]

## RESTRAINT, NOT GETTING OUR DESIRE

We, as a society in America, are no longer good at a discipline our forebears were much better at. The practice of restraint is something we struggle to understand. Ours is an instant society: instant oatmeal, fast food, movies on demand, instant gratification of all sorts. This instant culture seems to be fueled from within by a deep sense of entitlement, a characteristic sign of a narcissistic society. We want what we want and we want it now!

76 Geoffrey Bellman and Kathleen Ryan, *Extraordinary Groups: How Ordinary Teams Achieve Amazing Results* (San Francisco: Jossey-Bass, 2009), 27.

77 Ibid., 140.

We feel entitled to have it and will overcome any obstacle that threatens our wish fulfillment.

This supersized desire is a catalyst to the development of conflict. We clash with one another due to the perception that the other is standing in the way of us obtaining a rightful desire. The workplace can be the venue where people claw their way to the top. The antidote to this kind of self-centeredness is the older ideal of deferred gratification—self-restraint.

Part of a healthy team culture is a servant orientation, setting aside our own needs and considering the needs of others as greater than ourselves. This is a critical component to the success of a military unit. No one better understands the nobility of servanthood than the US armed forces. These heroes willingly put themselves in harm's way so that the rest of us, those they serve, can live in freedom and safety. Healthy teams in the workplace embody this selfless orientation as they restrain their own desire for gratification.

## RESISTANCE, NOT GIVING IN THROUGH CHARACTER

When several contributors for conflict are present, the impulse to activate either psychological defenses or evil tendencies heightens. Resisting our inner urges is the essence of character. We turn away from evil desires in light of our ethical principles and commitments. In a similar way, we turn away from defense mechanisms that will lead us toward conflict through the use of heightened emotional intelligence.

These two, ethics and emotional intelligence, in combination form our character. Character formed and forged over time has the ability to guide our judgment in critical situations approaching the threshold of conflict. Just as resistance in weight training builds better muscle mass and memory, so it is in this area of character. Exercise pays off. As we exercise our muscles of character with greater levels of resistance over time, our core strength is built.

## SYSTEMIC PREVENTION OF CONFLICT

The systemic life of the organization or team is driven by the ongoing development of culture. Every day the team is moving closer to or further from the culture to which they aspire. Culture is not an abstract or purely conceptual thing. It is actualized in the shared environment we cocreate.

Conflict is prevented in the system on a daily basis as each person in a team treats the others with deep care and respect. As we have demonstrated, it is very difficult to attack someone we rightly see as a valuable and indispensable asset to the team. In this key way, each member of the team has a part to play in prevention within the system.

Second, the system works toward prevention by dealing effectively with violations of core values. Companies with clear values of treating every member of the team with dignity do not tolerate violations of this expectation. Healthy systems deal quickly with potential breeches of these standards of conduct. The system, which holds the greatest power as a whole, is the greatest potential source of conflict prevention.

## CONFLICT IS LIKE FIRE

One helpful analogy that is useful to describe conflict prevention is fire. Fire requires the presence of certain essential components, namely fuel, air, and spark to ignite the initial flame. So it is with conflict. Conflict, like a forest fire, also occurs within a context. A well-managed forest reduces the risk of a catastrophic fire. To summarize the prevention strategies that we have been discussing, consider the following parallels between the creation of fire and the creation of conflict at all three levels.

**Table 4.** Conflict Prevention on Three Levels

| Levels of Potential Conflict | Components of Fire | Potential Conflict Components | Prevention Strategies |
|---|---|---|---|
| **ENVIRONMENTAL Factors** | Fuel / Air | Contributors:<br>• Humanness<br>• Lack<br>• Diversity (resistance to)<br>• Desire | Countered By:<br>• Responsibility<br>• Reciprocity<br>• Respect<br>• Restraint |
| **INTRAPERSONAL Factors** | Spark | Catalysts:<br>• Demand<br>• Devaluation<br>• Defenses<br>• Evil | Countered By:<br>• Resistance (character)<br>• Valuing others<br>• Increased EQ<br>• Ethics |
| **SYSTEMIC Factors** | Forest | Systemic Contribution:<br>• Inaction<br>• Covering up<br>• Willful blindness | Countered By:<br>• Active posture<br>• Zero tolerance<br>• Willingness to see |

In the same way that the devastation resulting from forest fires can be prevented, so the parallel devastation can and should be prevented in and among our teams and organizations. Smokey the Bear's words are true in the context of our teams. "Only you can prevent wildfires."

# 6

## CONFLICT RESOLUTION WHERE POSSIBLE

Have you ever tried to put toothpaste back into the tube? There is a point at which the attacks we sought to prevent occur. Like toothpaste out of a tube, putting it back the way it was is no longer possible. We can pretend that we don't see the mound of greenish-blue paste on the counter and even clean around this obstacle.

**At some point, it is time to clean up the mess and seek to put things back the way they are supposed to be to restore health and vitality.**

### WHEN THE LINE HAS BEEN CROSSED: AFTER THE DAMAGE

When situations escalate above the threshold of conflict, attacks have already happened. Damage has already been done. Prevention is always, for this obvious reason, preferred to resolution after the fact. Sometimes, however, our best efforts at prevention fail, and we are faced with the difficult task of resolving interpersonal conflicts on the team.

Indirect and direct attacks most often leave residual damage in their wake. Conflict resolution attempts to repair this damage to whatever extent possible. Damage that results from interpersonal conflict is of three main sorts: substantive, relational, and personal. Of these three, the substantive damage is far easier to restore to wholeness.

## SUBSTANTIVE ASPECTS

Many conflicts involve material or substantive issues. Take the example of a conflict that results in wrongful termination of an employee. This substantive damage may consist in lost wages, lost reputation, or unemployment. In other words, these are the more quantifiable aspects of conflict collateral damage. These are ordinarily things we can substantiate; we can quantify them at some level and seek to redress them once they are known.

## RELATIONAL ASPECTS

Relational aspects of conflicts are usually deeper, harder to understand, and much more difficult to heal. While emotions can run high in regard to substantive damages, it is normally relational aspects of conflict that drive the highest emotional charge. Human beings are inherently relational. This is the essence of what it means to be human. We are not only relational, we are emotional. Broken relationships that result from conflict cause us emotional pain. The deepest damage done as a result of relational breaches is typically at the level of the soul (*psyche*)—psychological damage.

## PERSONAL ASPECTS

Targets of conflict most often experience psychological or soul damage. It is common for victims of prolonged conflict to experience deep damage to their self-image and any number of psychologically driven symptoms that are results of their internal wounds. It is important to note that the damage they have suffered has been inflicted upon them from without. It is not a reflection on their strength or character.

# ESCALATING STRATEGIES FOR INTERVENTION

**Resolving conflict, at its best, brings wholeness and restoration to both sides of the equation, repairing substantive, relational, and personal brokenness.**

True conflict resolution results in the parties resuming genuine relationship, often at a level deeper than may have existed prior to the conflict. Conflict intervention strategies escalate to more people involved, greater costs, and higher stress levels. The further movement up the chain, the less direct control each party has over the outcome. Intervention begins with the personal level of conflict resolution, the individual self-aware enough to unilaterally move toward repairing things.

# LEVEL 1: PERSONAL RESPONSIBILITY

Level 1 intervention is at the intrapersonal level. At times, we become internally aware of damage we have done to a team member. We recognize the things we have done are serious enough that they will continue to cause damage to our relationship with the person we have offended. To seek the restoration of the relationship and to right damage done, we often need to simply step up to the plate and be honest. Key aspects of this level of intervention are:

## Self-Awareness

Self-awareness is a key aspect of character, the foundation of healthy teams. It is a component of higher levels of emotional intelligence and maturity. To be self-aware is to refuse to use un-healthy defense mechanisms to protect us from the knowledge that we have damaged a team member. Being self-aware renders us humble and vulnerable, willing to accept responsibility for our actions, without excuse.

## Responsibility / Ownership of Damage

When we own what we have done rather than feigning innocence, we have taken the first step toward potential resolution of the conflict. Our defenses are stubborn and persistent and hinder us from taking full ownership. At this level, we must individually overcome our internal demons that encourage us to cover up our mistakes.

## Restitution

To make restitution is to make every attempt to restore all that we have damaged. It includes efforts at restoring our opponent to substantive and relational wholeness as much as we are able. It is well said in the eighth and ninth steps of AA:

Step 8: Made a list of all persons we had harmed and became willing to make amends to them all.

Step 9: Made direct amends to such people wherever possible, except when to do so would injure them or others.

## Apology

To apologize is to own (without excuse) what has been done, to recognize its impact on a teammate, and to sincerely request forgiveness for the damage that remains after all has been done to make the teammate whole. Genuine apology never includes the words if, and, or but. It requests forgiveness rather than demanding it. If we can receive true forgiveness as a result of a sincere and humble request, the team can move back toward relational health. A clear and sincere apology has the potential to open this door.

## Stress Level

It is stressful to become vulnerable. Life has conditioned us to avoid this risk. When we have humbled ourselves and been honest in the past, perhaps we have suffered the consequences, some of which were undue. When conflict exists, damage has been done, and we will experience stress until the situation is repaired. This is normal and healthy. The stress level, as uncomfortable as it is at this level, only rises as we escalate toward greater intervention strategies. The best thing we can do to alleviate our stress when we have done wrong and caused damage is to simply be honest and own it.

# LEVEL 2: DYADIC (TWO-PERSON) INTERVENTION STRATEGIES

When we can't resolve conflict at level 1, we naturally escalate to level 2 strategies. Level 1 relies on the ability of the one who caused the damage to step forward unilaterally, owning his or her impact. Often, this does not occur. In such cases, level 2 becomes necessary. It begins with a renewed effort at mutual understanding and with a specific form of inquiry and confrontation.

## Mutual Understanding

At level 1, we are focused on understanding ourselves, correctly seeing how we have caused or contributed to the conflict situation. Moving up to level 2, we need to add to self-awareness an other-awareness, the understanding of others. Specifically, we are seeking to understand the ways in which the other person involved in the unresolved conflict is perhaps different than we are. Understanding them allows us to adapt for better communication and create a much greater potential for a successful outcome.

## Honest Inquiry (Soft Confrontation)

When people do not voluntarily own the damage they have done, it is sometimes necessary to help them understand. Confrontation is difficult to do well. Effective confronters require a good dose of humility. They need to recognize there may be much they do not understand about what actually transpired and most definitely about the underlying motives involved. Because of this reality, confrontation should most often take the form of honest, tentative inquiry, rather than hard, direct confrontation. It is always the case, as Ron has taught me, there are two experts in every conversation. I am the expert of the impact; the other person is the expert of his or her intent. This is a very helpful principle to remember at level 2.

## Interpersonal Forgiveness

Interpersonal forgiveness is a two-person transaction. It is a way of resolving unresolvable aspects of interpersonal conflict. Assuming that appropriate restitution has been pursued, that sincere apology has been offered, the damaged person is able to exercise forgiveness, to bear the cost in themselves of what remains. Healthy relationships over time rely on this ability to give and receive forgiveness for the inevitable offenses that occur in relationships.

## Relational Repair

Following the granting of forgiveness, the relationship has an opportunity (if both parties are willing) to move toward a new day relationally. With the resolution of the issues that have stood between the two parties, relationships are often able to move to new levels of trust and vulnerability over time. Successful conflict resolution is a boon to deeper relationships.

## Stress Level

It is stressful for most of us to attempt to make others aware of their impact on us and potential damage they have caused us personally. The stress level is lower at level 1, where the person doing the damage initiates the process of resolution. At level 2, the potential for encountering defenses and additional frustration is heightened. Nonetheless, dealing with conflict without a third party is preferred to the added stress that comes when we are unable to work out our differences on our own.

# LEVEL 3: TRIADIC (THIRD-PARTY) INTERVENTION STRATEGIES

It is common for the two parties in interpersonal conflict to be unable to resolve their conflict without the assistance of a third party. This frequently occurs in relationships ranging from marital to business partnerships and everything in between. The most difficult initial aspect of level 3 is often admitting our inability to solve the problem on our own.

## Third-Party Assistance

Third parties most often come from outside of the system. They form a relational bridge and buffer between the two conflicting parties and, if they are effective, are able to move both parties from dug-in positions toward a mutually beneficial process of resolution. The parties still retain a good measure of control over the outcome. The third-party facilitator can help assist both parties toward that end.

## Increased Safety

Conflict over time tends to increase our perceived lack of safety. Good third-party mediators are able to bring safety in the midst of high emotion. They bring a calming effect to the process. Their ability to listen well, to make both parties feel heard and validated, is essential to this sense of safety. Sometimes a significant power difference exists between the two primary parties in a dispute. This often precludes dyadic solutions to conflict. A third person can help balance power between the two parties and open up new doors of healthy interaction.

## Increased Objectivity

When conflicts rage, emotions run high. Subjectivity tends to rule the process. Good conciliators are able to do the hard work of objectifying the conflict. They do this by thoroughly gathering data on several levels:

- People Data (of all parties involved)
    - Behavioral Styles
    - Motivators
    - Emotional Intelligence
    - Family or Other Relevant History
- Conflict Data
    - Nature of Conflict (both parties perspectives + additional witnesses)
    - Timeline / History of Conflict (pertinent events over time)
    - Actual Damages
- System Data
    - Relevant Systemic Factors
    - Actions / Inactions of Authority Structures

Once adequate data is gathered and not before, the skilled conciliator can begin to formulate an assessment of the situation. The greatest need for any third-party facilitator is objectivity. The most needed skill is self-regulation, the ability to lessen overly emotional thinking, defer judgment, and delay conclusions.

## Improved Communication

In the midst of conflict, communication often breaks down. Third parties, through their effective listening, can assist both parties to open up. In addition, they often act as go-betweens, as interpreters who are able to convey messages from one party to the other in a way that can be received and understood.

In situations involving extremely broken communication, sometimes shuttle diplomacy can be utilized by conveying messages privately from one party to another through a third party. This strategy is sometimes necessary and helpful when the parties have escalated to the point that any face-to-face meetings will prove to be detrimental to obtaining a good outcome from the process. It creates a bridge for communication through an intermediary, so communication can continue without the stress that face-to-face communication would bring.

## Cost ($)

The costs associated with conflict in levels 1 and 2 are softer and more indirect. Conflict always costs, but the cost of conflict is not always observable on a financial report. Conflict over time takes a toll on hard-to-quantify things like employee engagement, morale, attendance, and other aspects of an emotionally distracted workforce.

The introduction of an outside third-party facilitator involves direct costs. The cost of not intervening at this level normally exceeds the cost of hiring help. Remember that the cost of un-resolved conflict in terms of the systemic effects can be great. All other team members and often the organization are being affected every day the situation continues as is.

## Stress Level

Mediation processes can be quite stressful, especially at the outset of the process. Oftentimes the stress level can be lowered as the mediator exerts a calming effect on all parties involved. People feel heard, perhaps for the first time in a long time. Hope of resolution often begins to emerge, leading to lowered levels of stress.

# INTERVENTION STRATEGIES WORTH AVOIDING IF POSSIBLE

Mediation is the preferred strategy to resolve disputes that have escalated beyond the ability of the parties to unilaterally or mutually resolve. It engages a third party to facilitate communi-cation and cooperation between the conflicting parties. When moving past level 3 strategies, the game changes quite rapidly.

# LEVEL 4: ARBITRATION

Arbitration involves the use of an arbitrator or judge to hear both sides of the case and render a verdict. Arbitration can be binding (what the judge says goes) or nonbinding (we may or may not follow the verdict), but in either case it is the decision of an outside third party that attempts to settle the dispute.

## Legal

Arbitration is a legal solution as opposed to a mutual and inter-personal one. It involves handing over evidence to a third party empowered by both parties to analyze data and offer findings.

## Third-Party Authority

At level 3, the third party is a facilitator. Both parties still maintain their ability to resolve the dispute themselves as assisted by the conciliator. At level 4, the third party moves from a position alongside the disputants to a place of authority over them both.

## Loss of Control

The locus of control shifts from the two parties assisted by the mediator to the arbitrator. The outcome rests solely on the arbitrator's judgment. As illustrated in Figure 10, the two parties, formerly bridged by a mediating third party, are now separated from one another and from the empowered third-party arbitrator. The control shifts drastically away from the parties to the authority.

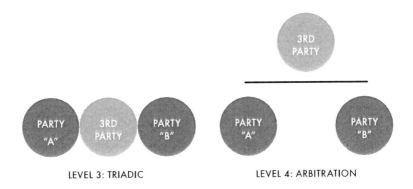

LEVEL 3: TRIADIC            LEVEL 4: ARBITRATION

**Figure 10.** Different locus of control from mediation to arbitration.

## Cost ($$)

Arbitration normally costs more than the alternative of media-tion. Both parties will normally incur legal expenses for repre-sentation during the arbitration proceedings. Normally these costs are not recoverable for either side.

## Stress Level

Due in part to a loss of control by shifting the locus to the arbi-trator, both parties will normally experience an increase in stress level beyond the stress of mediation. The arbitration process normally addresses only the substantive aspects of the conflict. The relationship at this point is usually unrecoverable, which adds another layer of stress to the process. Personal damages are not usually a part of the arbitration process.

# LEVEL 5: LITIGATION

Most contracts involve language that moves dispute resolu-tion away from litigation and toward mediation or arbitration. Litigation is costly and painful. It is and should be the last resort when it comes to unresolved conflicts. When litigation is pursued, the relational aspects of the conflict will likely never be restored. Relationships typically end when legal actions are undertaken.

All of this is not to say that legal action is not sometimes war-ranted. Occasionally, the only remedy available to resolve sub-stantive disputes is legal. This presupposes that one or both par-ties are unwilling or unable to participate in alternate dispute resolution processes (mediation/arbitration).

## Adversarial

Each side retains lawyers whose job it is to fight for their client. Within the law, each attorney is able to attack the credibility of the opposition. This fight tends to take a costly toll on both sides.

## Cost ($$$)

The cost of mediation looks small when comparing level 5 strategies. Litigation normally costs even more than arbitration, though sometimes legal costs can be recouped by the prevailing party. It is a high-stakes and extremely costly option.

## Stress Level

This is the most stressful of all available options and therefore to be reserved as a last resort only. The emotional toll of fighting an opponent in court is extremely high. Even if we prevail, the process exacts a high price from us.

Table 5 illustrates the escalating strategies involved in conflict resolution and should serve as a motivation for prevention as we consider the cost involved in intervention. At each level, the circle of people involved gets a bit larger and the costs (financial and other) increase.

**Table 5.** Escalating Conflict Intervention Strategies

| **LEVEL 5: LITIGATION** | • Legal<br>• Adversarial<br>• $$$<br>• Stress Level = 5 |
|---|---|
| **LEVEL 4: ARBITRATION** | • Legal<br>• Third-Party Authority<br>• Loss of Control<br>• $$<br>• Stress Level = 4 |
| **LEVEL 3: TRIADIC** | • Third-Party Assistance<br>• Objectivity<br>• Communication Improvement<br>• Mediation<br>• Power Balancing<br>• $<br>• Stress Level = 3 |
| **LEVEL 2: DYADIC** | • Honest Inquiry (Soft Confrontation)<br>• Interpersonal Forgiveness<br>• Relational Repair<br>• Stress Level = 2 |
| **LEVEL 1: PERSONAL** | • Humility<br>• Responsibility / Ownership<br>• Restitution<br>• Apology<br>• Stress Level = 1 |

Notice the bold line separating level 3 and 4. If at all possible, it behooves us to work toward conflict resolution at level 3 or below.

## UNRESOLVABLE CONFLICTS

*Imagine all the people, living life in peace.*

**— John Lennon**

Despite our best and most noble efforts and John Lennon's utopian dream, it appears that some conflicts in this life are un-resolvable. If we cannot accept this possibility, we will become slaves to this utopian idealism. Full conflict resolution is only possible with the full participation and ownership of all parties involved. If this participation cannot be achieved, full resolution no longer becomes possible.

**The responsibility to honestly acknowledge a conflict situation and attempt its resolution begins with each one of us.**

## OUR PERSONAL RESPONSIBILITY

If any of us involved from either side of a conflict situation re-fuses to participate in an equitable and forthright process, by default, the conflict will remain unresolved. We are only respon-sible for our own actions and cannot be responsible for the action or even inaction of others. If we have done all that we can reasonably do from our side of the table, and still the other party refuses to participate, we have faithfully carried out our personal duty.

To remain indefinitely connected to a conflict situation, waiting for an opponent to be willing to participate, is unhealthy. There is a need for adequate personal boundaries to prevent the drift toward codependence.

## THE WILLING PARTICIPATION OF OTHERS

It takes two to tango and it requires all parties to fully resolve conflict. We can fully commit to an honest participation in the process, but without the full engagement of others involved, our efforts at resolution will prove futile. We can drag them to the table through the use of threats or other strategies, but without their willing participation, desired results will not be reached.

Sometimes, parties initially less than willing to participate become fully engaged in the midst of the process and resolution becomes possible. Effective third-party facilitators can prove useful to engage the previously unwilling in the process.

## LIMITATIONS ON THE PROCESS

As demonstrated, the single most likely deterrent to conflict resolution is the unwillingness to participate on the part of one or both parties. Sometimes people participate outwardly but have failed to participate fully from the heart. This will prove deadly to obtaining a healthy outcome.

Conflict resolution is not always possible. This can prove to be quite disappointing for those of us who tend toward optimism. The stark reality of unresolved conflict offends us. We have a difficult time accepting the reality and are tempted to use various means at our disposal to pretend the remaining situation doesn't really exist.

# ACCEPTANCE

Coming to terms with the limitations of conflict intervention success is important when, despite our best efforts, our strategies fail to bring restoration. Like death, there are times when the best thing we can do to maintain our own emotional health is to accept the loss and to perhaps grieve the death of the relationship or the material losses. Acceptance of our inability to solve unresolvable conflict is a critical first step toward healing the deepest kind of damage, personal.

# CONCLUSION

## FACING OUR FEARS

Most of us have an aversion to conflict. This natural aversion may, however, not be in the best interest of team health. If our fears are crippling us and hindering us from dealing with the inevitable reality of organizational conflict, they must be squarely confronted. At great personal and team peril, we continue to deal ineffectively with conflict among us. To do nothing is to do something. To do nothing is to allow the status quo to drag us toward slow death. The fear that we hold on to is rarely spoken of. It is "that which we don't speak of" as if through denial and pretense we can avoid the effect of this fear. Quinn addressed this:

> Denial [*driven by fear of change*] occurs when we are presented with painful information about ourselves, information that suggests that we need to make a deep change. Denial is one of several clear paths toward slow death. When we practice denial, we work on the wrong solutions or no solutions at all [*doing nothing*]. The problem grows worse as we become discouraged, and our vitality level declines.[78]

Not speaking of our fear is an attempt to control it. However, by not speaking of it, we actually empower it and allow it, quietly and unnoticed, to control us.

---

78 Quinn, *Deep Change*, 52 (italics added).

**There is much about the human condition in conflict that is ugly, things we would rather not see, particularly in ourselves.**

If this premise is correct, however, our refusal to look at these indications of ill health will perpetuate the same results. If a deeper understanding of the path toward conflict disarms it somehow, we should continue the conversation as a team, to deeply discuss the myriad ways that conflict gains a foothold in our shared work life and to together resolve to prevent it at every point along the path of development.

Your work as a team begins with an honest self-assessment of your present level of conflict prevention effectiveness. Potential conflict contributors are fuel (wood, paper, gasoline) waiting for a spark to ignite them into flame. Take the self-assessment in the following pages (discuss your findings with each other) to enter into a topic that you may need to mutually confess you have been collectively avoiding.

# TEAM CONFLICT PREVENTION CHECKLIST

*(check all that apply)*

## RESPONSIBILITY (HUMANNESS)

❏  I take full responsibility for damage I have caused to others.

❏  I do not appeal to my humanness as an excuse for things I have done that have damaged others.

❏  We are cocreating a culture that doesn't allow our humanity to be used as an excuse for our bad behavior.

❏  We have a practiced culture of responsibility in our organization.

## RECIPROCITY (LACK)

❏  When I see others in need around me and have the resources to help, I do what I can.

❏  If I can't personally help, I seek to inform others who can help with the need.

❏  As a team, we help others in their areas of weakness or need. We don't use their weaknesses against them.

❏  We are cocreating a culture of giving and serving others.

## RESPECT (DIVERSITY)

❏  I am growing in my ability to respect and value others who differ from me in significant ways.

❏  I am aware of remaining areas of intolerance and bias within me.

❏  We are cocreating a culture of respect and of valued diversity.

☐ We regularly discuss the benefits of our differences and encourage the free exchange of different opinions, thoughts, and ideas.

## RESTRAINT (DESIRE)

☐ I regularly practice the healthy discipline of restraining my desire when it is for the sake and benefit of the team.

☐ I sincerely believe that what I want is not the most important thing in many team decisions.

☐ We are cocreating a culture of appropriate deferred gratification and healthy restraint.

☐ We all regularly yield to the desires of others on the team.

## RESISTANCE
## (EVIL, DEFENSE MECHANISMS, DEVALUATION)

☐ I am aware of my commonly utilized defense mechanisms that signal a perceived threat to my ego.

☐ I regularly catch myself if and when I attempt to use unhealthy defense mechanisms.

☐ I am able to use emotional self-regulation to avoid doing or saying something I'll regret later.

☐ I am aware of my own propensity for evil behavior.

☐ I am aware when I begin to devalue others in my mind.

☐ I am determined to advocate for those who are being devalued around me.

☐ We have a good understanding of defense mechanisms and are able to alert each other when using them inappropriately or destructively.

☐ We don't allow people to displace emotions and project motives onto others on the team.

- ☐ We have moral courage as a team to stand up to evil behavior on the team.
- ☐ We have zero tolerance toward mistreatment or abuse of others on the team.
- ☐ We call each other on statements that devalue others.
- ☐ We affirm the unique value of each person on the team and his or her right to always be treated with human dignity and respect.

## SYSTEMIC PREVENTION

- ☐ We have clear antibullying policies in our organization.
- ☐ We all agree to stand together to hold those who mistreat others accountable for their behavior.
- ☐ We agree not to silently condone the mistreatment of others.
- ☐ We agree never to be part of covering up or hiding the mistreatment of others.

## UNRESOLVABLE CONFLICTS

- ☐ I recognize my limits as they pertain to resolving all conflicts.
- ☐ I will not give up on resolving a conflict until I have done all I can reasonably do to try to resolve it.

# PART 2

## MOVING TOWARD HEALTH

# INTRODUCTION

# ORGANIZATIONAL ENTROPY

Something we may not remember from junior high or high school science class is the principle of entropy as it relates to the second law of thermodynamics. Isaac Asimov expressed this principle this way:

> Another way of stating the second law then is, *"The universe is constantly getting more disorderly!"* Viewed that way we can see the second law all about us. We have to work hard to straighten a room, but left to itself it becomes a mess again very quickly and very easily. Even if we never enter it, it becomes dusty and musty. How difficult to maintain houses, and machinery, and our own bodies in perfect working order: how easy to let them deteriorate. In fact, all we have to do is nothing, and everything deteriorates, collapses, breaks down, wears out, all by itself—and that is what the second law is all about.[79]

You naturally understand the principle of entropy, whether you use the technical term or not; you know intuitively that a system is not going to gain more organization, health, or wholeness unless energy is put into it. Things don't get better, healthier, more developed on their own. Energy has to be put into the system to create greater levels of order and meaning. Buildings

---

79 Isaac Asimov, "In the Game of Energy and Thermodynamics You Can't Even Break Even," *Smithsonian Institution Journal* (June 1970), 6 (italics added).

don't naturally construct themselves—a team of designers and builders spends months bringing the creative vision to realization. Plants do not just naturally grow—they must have energy from the sun, adequate water, care, and protection from disease and pests (weeds are another story).

This world is inevitably running down. This is a law (an inviolable principle), which is fairly easy for most people to grasp. We all realize that things will decay over time unless we actively maintain them. Organizations, as living systems, cannot adapt toward health unless outside energy is added into the system. This energy must often come in the form of much more dramatic changes to paradigms, as opposed to minor or incremental ones. This is the theory of Robert Quinn. He explained organizational entropy in the following way:

> Organization and change are not complementary concepts. To organize is to systematize, to make behavior predictable. All organizations are based on systems of external and internal expectations. . . . All these expectations help ensure predictable behavior. . . . As time goes on, however, *these routine patterns move the organization toward decay and stagnation.* The organization loses alignment with the changing, external reality. . . . *The organization faces a choice: either adapt or take the road to slow death.*[80]

According to this principle of entropy, "moving toward slow death," any organization that does nothing in terms of added energy (think organizational development energy) will tend to simply run down, moving increasingly toward deeper levels of disorder and decay. This explains why organizations that are not actively seeking to grow will not simply remain at status quo but will actually regress.

---

80 Quinn, *Deep Change*, 5 (italics added).

Quinn's theory is that deep change happens in the midst of a crisis. Often, this is the case, particularly with team leaders who lead better in crisis mode (high Ds). This is not universal, however. Other teams defy slow death through just as radical, yet steady, change over time. They resist entropy as a longer sustained effort. In both ways, then, teams work together toward effecting a paradigm shift. With or without the crisis, the net results are critical for ongoing growth and development as an organization.

If this is true, why then do so few companies and organizations put forth energy (in the form of strategies and budgets) toward the development of their employees as individuals and the team as a system?

**If we do not infuse life, health, and strength into the system, regression will be the logical outcome of our neglect.**

To do nothing is to do something. Not acting has predictable outcomes.

Top tier organizations recognize this principle and are therefore willing to put energy toward organizational development and health. Why would they do this? Doesn't that cut into the profits of the organization? In fact, it can be demonstrated that it not only does *not* reduce profits in the long run but it significantly improves them. The logical question for us to ask ourselves in response is one of self-evaluation. How much energy are we or our organization committing toward the goal of minimizing entropy? Do we truly value team and organizational health?

Some have attempted to defy natural laws. The interesting reality is that these built-in principles always win. We can attempt to defy gravity, but our visit to the emergency room confirms its ever-present reign. So it is with organizations and entropy. We either do what is required to actively resist decline or we passively move toward disorganization and slow organizational death. The principles are unchanging. The choice, however, for our organization and our team is ours. As Quinn reminded us,

> Energy is neither created nor destroyed. At any given moment, it flows toward some points in the universe and away from others. The amount of energy we feel has much to do with the alignment between ourselves and our surrounding environment. We can be aligned with our environment in such a way that we feel either strong and empowered or weak and powerless.[81]

In the end the question remains, what are you and your team willing to do to resist entropy? If you are willing to put in the requisite work, entropy can be defied. This can only happen in healthy teams.

---

81 Quinn, *Deep Change*, 41.

# 7

## WHAT IS A HEALTHY TEAM?

The concept of teams has been in vogue in the corporate American culture since at least the mid-1980s. After over thirty years of seeking to derive meaning from this term, have we exhausted its potential? Perhaps not. This second section will begin by forming and giving shape to this concept of "team." What is a team, as opposed to other recently proposed alternative terms? And, more importantly, what constitutes a "healthy" team? If team health is the most important thing to pursue, we need to describe these parameters of team well-being.

## WHAT WE CALL OURSELVES

Our language matters. Language gives shape to team culture and outlook. The terms we use to describe ourselves and our group identity reveal many aspects of who we are and where we are going. For this reason, a clearer definition of each of the frequently used terms will help frame our discussion of the concept of team. Three terms dominate the current landscape:

# ORGANIZATIONS

Organizations, though composed of people, are famous for being impersonal and faceless. BusinessDictionary.com defines an organization as:

> A social unit of people that is *structured* and *managed* to meet a need or to pursue collective goals (italics added).

When we use the term organization, we are referring to an entity with particular regard to the way it is structured and managed (organized).[82] The organizational chart is a graphic representation of the structure and hierarchy within a business. It typically portrays the distribution of power and authority but does not address many of the aspects of healthy team dynamics.

As organizations get larger, they move further away from the ability to function as a singular team or group. Simultaneously, they often move further away from working through personal relationships and instead move toward working through policies and procedures (structures) as the primary means of running the organization. As size increases, so do complexity and the need for more layers of structure and the means to maintain that structure and assure quality results management. This is where the potential for organizational "slow death" that Quinn warned of enters. People can get lost in the midst of overorganized culture. This is the substance of the cartoon *Dilbert*.

Organizations of any size have cultures and personalities. Larger organizations are typically comprised of various working groups or teams, sometimes called departments or silos. This reality of separate teams or tribes within an organization can often lead to

---

82 The term company is often used similarly and carries much of the same connotation (and baggage). Company normally refers to a for-profit business organization, whereas the more general term can refer to both for-profits and nonprofits.

internal conflict, silo rivalry, and competition. Successful healthy organizations are able to effectively unify the teams that comprise them around shared big picture clarity.

The term **organization** speaks of the distribution of power, authority, and accountability. It carries the torch of management and structure.

## TRIBES

Tribe is a cultural term describing the way a group or team connects around shared values and beliefs. From the earliest days of humankind, people have been organized in tribes, traditionally groups with a shared tribal ancestry, culture, and heritage. The tribe was an extended family. This shared lineage idea of tribe has been eroded in part in the United States as a result of the great American melting pot. Tribal cultures brought by immigrants have given way to a new blended cultural context. This has set the stage for the need to be part of a new kind of tribe, an ideological one.

Seth Godin described a tribe as "a group of people connected to one another, connected to a leader, and connected to an idea."[83] Godin emphasized that due to the increasing connectedness of the planet, a tribe is no longer restricted by physical boundaries. Being part of a tribe answers our deep desire to belong, to be identified with something and someone we can believe in. The organization as a whole can function as a tribe or there can be several differing tribes housed within a larger organization's structure.

In the same year that Godin wrote *Tribes*, Dave Logan, John King, and Halee Fischer-Wright identified a *tribe* as a group of 20 to

---

83 Seth Godin, *Tribes: We Need You to Lead Us* (New York: Penguin, 2008), 1.

150 people who are connected (you have them in your contact list) and unified by a common language and common cultural values. Their model includes five stages of tribal development under the influence of tribal leaders:[84]

**Table 6.** Tribal Stages, Team Building, and Potential Conflict in an Organization

| Tribal Stage | Key Characteristics | Key Phrase | Team-Building Opportunity | Prevalence of Conflict |
|---|---|---|---|---|
| **Stage 1** (2%) | • Like a street gang<br>• Survival mode<br>• Getting through an unfair life | "Life sucks." | None | High |
| **Stage 2** (25%) | • Dunder-Mifflin<br>• Chronic complaint<br>• Skepticism | "My life sucks." | None | High |
| **Stage 3** (44%) | • Competitive<br>• Individualistic | "I'm great (and you're not)." | None | High |
| **Stage 4** (22%) | • Shared pride<br>• Common foe | "We're great (and they're not)." | Great | Low |
| **Stage 5** (2%) | • Pure vision<br>• No competitor | "Life is great." | Great | None |

The five stages describe levels of tribal culture that are readily identifiable upon examination of tribal language. The tribe builds its culture with the language it utilizes.[85]

84 Dave Logan, John King, and Halee Fischer-Wright, *Tribal Leadership: Leveraging Natural Groups to Build a Thriving Organization* (New York: HarperCollins, 2008).

85 For this reason, the New Suggested Terms (a glossary of tribal language) was placed at the front of the book in an easy-to-access reference location.

According to Logan et al., tribal stages of organizations fall in a near-normal distribution. Very few teams rise to their stage 5 and only the healthiest elevate to stage 4. Moving team culture to level 4 is key. As you can see, tribes at level 3 or below have a volatile mix of high probability for conflict and virtually no opportunity for healthy team development. For this reason, the bulk of the comments in this book are reliant on the development of at least stage 4 tribal culture. Without that, health will continue to elude our teams. Individualistic thinking and apathy at lower stages predict conflict and preclude health. Where team leaders are unwilling to move toward a stage 4 culture, the possibility for real health rapidly vanishes.

The metaphor of the tribe greatly informs the discussion of team health and culture. **Tribes** are about culture, beliefs, meaning, and significance.

## GROUPS

Bellman and Ryan defined a group as "a collection of individuals, typically of two to about twenty, who come together around a common purpose." They go on to describe what they refer to as extraordinary groups:

> [*They*] achieve outstanding results, and members—individually or collectively—experience a profound shift in how they see their world; they are transformed.[86]

Their emphasis falls on the adjective *extraordinary* as they described the way these groups of individuals are transformed through peak shared experiences. Bellman and Ryan's group is tribal in the way it uses common language and shared values to move toward these life-changing and life-shaping occurrences.

---

86 Bellman and Ryan, *Extraordinary Groups*, 11 (italics added).

**Groups** speak of our desire to belong. They are about security and connection, about the sharing of lives that gives meaning.

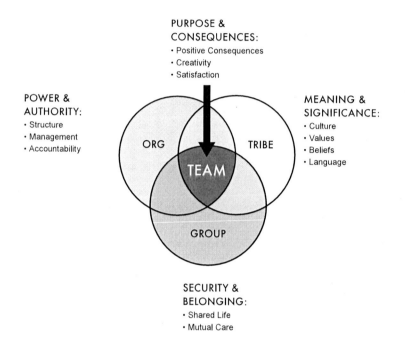

**Figure 11.** Team combines aspects of group, tribe, and organization.

## TEAM

The term **team** embodies aspects of the nature of organizations, tribes, and groups and adds the emphases of fulfilling a common purpose and together creating positive consequences (results). Team occurs at the intersection of these three types of groupings. It is, therefore, an inclusive term large enough to wrap into itself various significant aspects of organizations, groups, and tribes. What then constitutes a team?

# THE ESSENCE OF TEAM

At a bare minimum, any team embodies certain fundamental attributes. Any group of individuals with less than these is not rightly called a team. Consider the following definition of the essence of a team:

*A team is an identifiable, rightly sized, organized, and interconnected group of members that operates according to certain team rules and pursues common objectives.*

- **Identifiable.**

    A team is always identifiable. Sports teams use rosters and uniforms to mark out this boundary. We know who is on the team by virtue of their inclusion or exclusion from the roster or the color of their respective jersey. Teams of all sorts always have boundaries that determine them. If I am a member of team X, I am not a member of team Y.[87]

- **Rightly sized.**

    What's the right size for a team? It depends. For many sports teams the size is dictated by the rules of the game. In the workplace, size varies dependent upon the nature of the team and the reason for its existence. We know a team is too big when it does not allow the active and meaningful participation of all team members. We know it is too small when we lack the diversity and synergy that comes with the addition of team members. In any case, there is most often a right size for the team as determined either from within or from without.

---

87 Where different teams overlap within the organization, belonging to several teams may be applicable. It is, however, no less critical for each of us to know which team(s) we are on.

- **Organized.**

  Teams require organization. By definition, an unorga-
  nized group of people does not constitute a team. Sports
  teams spend hours together strategizing and practicing
  to perfect their ability to work as a team. This requires
  various kinds and levels of organization. Each player
  needs to know his or her role and function as part of the
  team. Without this fundamental understanding, chaos
  ensues.[88]

- **Interconnected.**

  All teams are connected as a group. Together, they, for
  better or worse, form a system. This team connection
  may be as weak as sharing the same uniform, lining up
  on the same side of the field, or banding together to survive an abusive coach. Even in these ways, connections
  (albeit weak) exist. A disconnected group of individuals
  does not constitute a team.

- **Team rules (norms).**

  Every team has certain rules that govern its behavior as
  a group. There are certain norms and group expectations that are essential to the nature of a team. Keeping
  team rules is normally enforced by the group, as well as
  enforcing agreed-upon consequences when team rules
  are violated.

- **Common objectives.**

  For sports teams, this often means winning. The common
  objectives of the team are those things that are readily

---

88 Imagine a football team breaking the huddle with no idea who is playing which
position.

identified as the reason to assemble as a team. No objective, no team.

These six essential elements characterize teams of all sorts. Where one or more of these are lacking, the term team may be misapplied to a group. These traits together constitute a minimal definition of team. Unhealthy teams can possess all of these attributes. However, the focus here is in differentiating between unhealthy, mediocre teams and healthy, vital, significant teams.

## HEALTHY TEAMS

Teams, of many shapes and sizes, of many degrees of health or dysfunction, of varying levels of positive results, exist. What is the earmark of a superior team? What is the target we are striving for together as a team? Many experts in the field of organizational development agree that the focus on *organizational health is the key factor that trumps all others.* Patrick Lencioni said,

> Once organizational health is properly understood and placed into the right context, it will surpass all other disciplines in business as the greatest opportunity for improvement and competitive advantage. Really.[89]

As it goes for the larger organization, so it goes for the team. Team health and team dysfunction are at two opposite ends of the continuum.

**The goal for any team is to be continually moving toward health. If health is not pursued, the default results will be dysfunction and conflict.**

---

89 Patrick Lencioni, *The Advantage: Why Organizational Health Trumps Everything Else in Business* (San Francisco: Jossey-Bass, 2012), 4.

What then comprises team health? We need to expand our minimal definition of team. In addition to the minimum aspects shared by all teams, **healthy teams** can be defined as follows:

*A healthy team is an identifiable, rightly sized, well-organized, strongly interconnected, group of securely attached members in vital relationship with each other, who share common tribal language, culture, core values, and beliefs, who operate in accordance with them, and who clearly understand individual and group roles and core purposes that together cocreate positive consequences of all sorts.*

- **Healthy.**

  Health is a broad term that describes the overall well-being of the team and its individuals. Too often, organizational teams measure their success by the narrow metrics of financial profit or market share.[90] As we unpack the positive consequences that are both the means and the end of healthy teams, we will find that health is all-inclusive.[91]

- **Well-organized.**

  Bellman and Ryan's model of extraordinary groups informs us here. They spoke of the sweet spot of "just enough structure." Overstructuring or understructuring misses this mark.

  [*Extraordinary groups*] will establish and honor systems, plans, roles, tasks, and working agreements—*if* those structures fit the challenges ahead of them. But they never forget that the

90 These are the "carrots" of motivation 2.0 and 2.1 as described by Daniel Pink in *Drive: The Surprising Truth about What Motivates Us.*
91 See chapter 12, Positive Consequences.

main reason they are together is about fulfilling their purpose. The structure is a means to that end.[92]

Structure, organization, and management are a means to a greater end, not the end itself. Healthy teams are organized well, in a way that best serves overall team health and cultivates positive consequences.

- **Strongly interconnected.**

  All teams are connected. Healthy teams are connected in specific ways that not only reflect internal health but propel the team forward to greater shared results. Healthy teams share strong bonds of trust and mutual respect. These bonds serve them well when stress or adversity challenges team connection.[93]

- **Securely attached.**

  Related to the strong bonds of trust and mutual respect, healthy teams experience safety and security as valued members of the team. Their deep sense of belonging and acceptance allows them to venture into increasingly creative and potentially vulnerable areas within the safety of a healthy team environment, a safe base.

- **Vitally related.**

  Healthy teams share a vital relationship with one another. Clear, helpful communication is the means by which they stay in relationship and keep moving forward. We've all seen examples of sports teams where the all-stars as-

92 Bellman and Ryan, *Extraordinary Groups*, 24 (italics added).

93 See chapter 9, Strong Cohesiveness.

sembled clearly don't like each other. Healthy teams are the opposite of this dynamic.[94]

- **Culturally connected.**

   Healthy teams have clarity about their shared language, culture, core values, and beliefs. They have invested time together to come to a common, well-thought-out consensus that serves to unify them as a team.[95]

- **Congruently behaved.**

   Healthy teams don't just talk about their shared values and purposes; they live in accordance with them. They guard against the development of a gap between aspirational and practiced values. They seek to practice what they preach and to interact with one another and with those they serve with integrity, congruence, and wholeness.[96]

- **Clear.**

   Healthy teams are laser focused on their common purpose, their individual roles, their shared values and beliefs, and their core business definition. They stay focused on these marks they have established together.[97]

- **Cocreating positive consequences.**

   Healthy teams cocreate the "good life" they seek after together. They value all aspects of positive team conse-

---

94 See chapter 11, Clear Communication.

95 See chapter 10, Laser Clarity.

96 See chapter 8, Shared Character.

97 See chapter 10, Laser Clarity.

quences and seek to succeed at all levels of team health including:[98]

- Job satisfaction
- Sense of fulfillment
- Joy in working together for meaningful ends
- Financial rewards and profitability
- Rich, satisfying relationships with team members
- Increased freedom from the draining effects of conflict
- Lowered levels of stress and improved physical health
- Improved emotional and psychological health
- Higher levels of engagement and experience of flow

## BLENDING INDIVIDUAL AND COLLABORATIVE EFFORTS

Tennis teams differ from basketball. One does individual work, plays singles or doubles matches, and adds up the collective score at the end of the day. The other plays together in such a way that all members of the team are actually touching the one ball as the team plays as a unit. The basketball team works collaboratively and either wins or loses collectively. Single tennis players can win all of their individual matches, and the team can still lose the match. For many years, the basketball type of team has been advocated from the public school system to the office. It has more recently been demonstrated that this collaborative-heavy sense of team may not produce the best results in the workplace.

98 See chapter 12, Positive Consequences.

In reality, healthy working teams are somewhere between these two pictures. At times, teams must work collaboratively. At other times, the results that only come from intense individual pursuit are what the team needs as a whole. The comparison to sports teams is inadequate to fully describe the way a working team conducts itself. Sports are played within a fairly tight time frame in a public arena and are primarily driven by the prize of winning the game. Work teams strive together over a much longer time period, largely unnoticed by others and only in part for the pursuit of winning, financial success, or profitability.

Further, sports teams (in team sports as opposed to individual team sports like golf, tennis, or swimming) must accomplish their goals as a unit. They all must cooperate and work exclusively together, never truly independently. Susan Cain helped to point out the fallacy of directly applying this sense of teamwork to the nonsports pursuit of shared success. She criticized the New Groupthink described as

> [A model] which holds that creativity and achievement come from an oddly gregarious place. Most of us now work in teams, in offices without walls, for managers who prize people skills above all. Lone geniuses are out. Collaboration is in.[99]

She adeptly reminded us that working always in groups and never as individuals does not produce the greatest team results and creativity. Healthy teams appropriately balance between working collaboratively and independently, even as they seek to maintain their core qualities.

---

99 Susan Cain, "The Rise of the New Groupthink," *The New York Times* (January 13, 2012): accessed July 31, 2013, http://nytimes.com/2012/01/15/opinion/sunday/the-rise-of-the-new-groupthink.html?_r =0&pagewanted=print (italics added).

# EXISTING MODELS OF TEAMS

The development of the workplace team as an organizing principle has existed in seminal form since the Hawthorne Studies
conducted by Elton Mayo in the 1930s. As a leader in the
Human Relations Movement, he and others began to see that
performance was dependent on the combination of job content (results) and social issues (teamwork). Teams characterized
the working groups that became normative in the mid-1980s
among America's top companies. In the history of team model
development, a few are worth noting for our purposes.

# SELECT HISTORY OF TEAM MODELS

## Katzenbach and Smith (1993)—High-Performance Team Model

In *The Wisdom of Teams*, Jon Katzenbach and Douglas Smith presented a model of high-performance teams as the pinnacle of several stages of teams or pseudoteams as follows:

- **Working group:** a group with a need or opportunity that is not really trying to be a team.

- **Pseudoteam:** a group with a need or opportunity that is not really trying to be a team.

- **Potential team:** a group with a need or opportunity, trying to improve its team performance but lacks clarity and accountability.

- **Real team:** a small group of people with complementary skills who are committed to a common purpose, goals, and culture for which they hold themselves accountable.

- **High-performance team:** real team plus team members who are deeply committed to one another's personal growth and success.[100]

## Lencioni (2002)—Five Dysfunctions Model

Patrick Lencioni defined functional teams by describing a fivefold model of team dysfunction. The dysfunctions were arranged hierarchally from the bottom up as follows:[101]

- Absence of trust

- Fear of conflict

---

100 Team-type descriptions derived from Jon Katzenbach and Douglas Smith, *The Wisdom of Teams: Creating the High-Performance Organization* (New York: HarperCollins, 1999), 91–92.

101 Patrick Lencioni, *The Five Dysfunctions of a Team: A Leadership Fable* (San Francisco: Jossey-Bass, 2002).

- Lack of commitment

- Avoidance of accountability

- Inattention to results

### Bellman and Ryan (2009)—Extraordinary Groups Model

"An extraordinary group achieves outstanding results while members experience a profound shift in how they see their world."[102] Geoffrey Bellman and Kathleen Ryan described eight traits of extraordinary groups:

- A compelling purpose

- Shared leadership

- Just-enough structure

- Full engagement

- Embraced differences

- Unexpected learning

- Strengthened relationships

- Great results

### Lencioni (2012)—Four Disciplines of Healthy Organizations Model

Patrick Lencioni recently proposed a four-discipline model of organizational health:[103]

- Build a cohesive leadership team

  - Build trust

  - Master conflict

  - Achieve commitment

---

102 Bellman and Ryan, *Extraordinary Groups*, 17.

103 Lencioni, *The Advantage*.

- Embrace accountability

- Focus on results

• Create clarity

    - Why we exist

    - How we behave

    - What we do

    - How we will succeed

    - What is most important right now

    - Who must do what

  • Overcommunicate clarity

  • Reinforce clarity

### Price (2004–2013)—Disciplines of Extraordinary Teams Model

Ron Price's model of Extraordinary Teams as he has taught it for several years with a few variations is essentially as follows:

  • Build cohesiveness

  • Develop / maintain organizational clarity

  • Communicate effectively

  • Manage for performance

  • Improve continuously and systemically

All of the previous models contribute valuable insights into the qualities of healthy and effective teams. Synthesizing aspects of each of these models, along with helpful additions and clarifications, the following is proposed:

## THE HEALTHY TEAM MODEL

A healthy, and therefore effective, team is a group of individuals that are functionally interconnected for the purpose of achieving mutually desired team results. Healthy teams can be shown to embody five key characteristics as illustrated below.

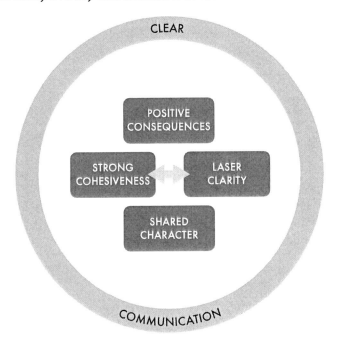

**Figure 12.** The Healthy Team Model.

The healthy team embodies five key qualities organized as follows:

- **Shared character** is the foundation of the team and of each individual on the team.

- **Strong cohesiveness** bonds teammates to one another, creating a healthy environment. (Cohesiveness and clarity are reciprocal; they are cocreated.)

- **Laser clarity** regarding the critical questions is shared by each group member and the whole.

- **Positive consequences** are the result (end) of the health of the team and the driver (means) to future results.

- **Clear communication** is the means of relationship and forms the boundary of the team, holding the team together.

The Healthy Team Model reflects the reality of healthy teams, which are

- **Stable** as reflected by the building blocks in the midst of the model with character as foundational and positive consequences as the capstone.

- **Dynamic** as reflected by the wheel of team communication that reflects the ongoing need for the system to be moved toward greater health and positive consequences.

The Healthy Team Model, in its five components, forms the outline for the remainder of Part 2. Before we move on to the foundation of shared character, there is one additional and critical aspect of healthy teams that needs to be mentioned.

## THE NEED FOR A COACH

Coaching matters. The elite collegiate coaches of the NCAA are able year after year, with students graduating from their programs annually, to put together top-ranked teams. That is why universities are willing to pay large sums of money to attract the best coaches to their programs. It is almost inconceivable to think of Duke basketball without Mike Krzyzewski, or Boise

State football without Chris Peterson.[104] Coaches really do make programs.

In contrast, some other sports teams have rather unsuccessfully tried to use player–coaches. A player–coach is an individual who appears on the team roster as both a player and a coach. He or she wears two hats. One of the intrinsic difficulties with this concept revolves around role clarity. When the coach is on the floor or in the game, is he or she a player or the coach? This role confusion, among other problems, has relegated the idea of player–coaches to an anomaly.

It is not infrequent for a major league baseball manager to be ejected from a ball game. Baseball teams can survive and even sometimes prevail over an opponent while being coachless for the remainder of a game. This is only a temporarily sustainable pattern. No team will do well in the long run without the vital leadership that a coach provides. It would be unthinkable for a sports team to attempt to compete without a coach. Yet, in the business world, the inclusion of coaches, whether in-house or outside, has not been as normalized as perhaps it should be.

Successful teams have clearly defined roles. The role of coach differs from the role of player. Yet both are critical for team success. As it is for sports teams, so it is in organizations. Coaches, who closely interact with the individuals and their systems, are often uniquely outside of the system, providing the following benefits for healthy teams:

- Assessment of current team and individual traits and talents

104 Chris Peterson announced his departure for the University of Washington just prior to the printing of this book. We can expect his coaching impact to make the program there as it has at Boise State.

- Objectivity (emotional distance)

- Group discussion facilitation

- Outside feedback for individuals

- Catalysts for systemic change, status quo questioners

- Third-party assistance in conflict (mediation ability)

- Strategy development

- Performance monitoring

- Accountability

- Instruction and teaching

- Personal, team, and organizational development

An executive coach, a professional who works with individuals and teams in a business context, blends acumen in four critical areas:

- **Business knowledge:** understanding of business principles, practices, and strategies as applied to the context of organizations and teams.

- **Psychological knowledge:** understanding of psychological principles and theories as applied to the context of organizations and teams.

- **Organizational (systems) knowledge:** understanding of system and organizational developmental theory as applied in the context of organizations and teams.

- **Coaching knowledge:** understanding of the main theories and modalities of coaching and consulting with organizations and teams.

Coaching occurs at the intersection of these four disciplines. It is a unique blend of hard and soft sciences with a whole lot of additional wisdom and knowledge that allows the effective coach to work primarily in the present with a focus on the future health and success of the organizational client.

The executive coach and similar coaching professionals assist the team in the development of the softer skills (conflict prevention and team building) reflected in this book. This outside influence and instruction are combined with expertise and understanding of the harder sciences of economics, business, and organizational development to create a unique relationship that benefits the team holistically.

The coaching relationship, unlike others that are common in the workplace, is a "do with" relationship. It is substantially different than other less helpful business relationships that can be characterized as "do to" or "do for."[105] It is a strategic partnership aimed at bringing team health, with all of its benefits, increasingly into fruition. To have a healthy, vital, and even a winning team, we need to have a good coach. What I admire most about Chris Peterson at Boise State isn't his winning percentage, which is among the best in NCAA history, but the way he sincerely seeks to develop character in each of the young men he has the privilege to influence. Character is the foundation that will serve them for years to come after they leave the blue turf of Boise. So it is for your team as well.

## A THINKING PARTNER

Healthy teams and leaders recognize their need for outside objectivity to counter the great potential for willful blindness and

---

105 See Ron Ernst, *RealTime Coaching*.

groupthink within the organization. It is very difficult for those inside of the organization to give good, objective, or difficult feedback, particularly to their superiors. Everyone in the organization, at some level, has some degree of a personal agenda.

**Teams and organizations are famous for having cats in bags, elephants in the room, and sacred cows.**

The identification of these unspoken hindrances to team performance and health opens up new areas of discussion and potential for moving toward greater future results.

People within the system with a stake to protect are at a disadvantage when it comes to their ability to see and provide feedback to the group. Outside coaches and consultants for teams provide an essential level of feedback that is not biased by internal group dynamics in the way that insiders must be. Great leaders look for this outside influence to help their teams expose elephants in the room. They realize that outside professionals who partner with them for the best interest of the organization are more able to provide the critical input they need to succeed. Margaret Heffernan, who successfully ran several organizations in the role of CEO, validated the need for a third, outside opinion:

> You need a third opinion that comes from someone who has nothing but your best interests, the company's best interests, at heart. That person is a thinking partner. Not someone who knows the answer [*nor imposes it*] but someone who thinks alongside with you in order to find it.[106]

It is this third-party objectivity that coaches provide to healthy teams that are desirous of avoiding the all-too-common pitfalls. Great teams have great coaches, individuals gifted at helping them think more clearly.

---

106 Heffernan, *Willful Blindness*, 227 (italics added).

# 8

## SHARED CHARACTER

At the beginning of the twenty-first century in America, we find ourselves in a crisis. It is deeper than just the economic recession that began in 2008 and continues to resist full recovery. It is deeper than the threats of global terrorism. It is a crisis of character. In the last fifty years and more, we have witnessed the erosion of this most precious commodity in almost all spheres of our existence. Donovan Campbell, author and marine, lamented,

> [I]nstitutions that define our views of ourselves and of our country, among them business and government [*add religious institutions and the family*], have lost substantial credibility. Their leaders are largely viewed as greedy, selfish, hypocritical, criminal, shortsight-

ed, incompetent, or all of the above. This widespread destruction of trust has left a leadership vacuum that is slowly becoming filled with despair. . . . Many of the leaders we trusted have been revealed as cheaters, criminals, or incompetents. We have lost faith in our leaders, and when faith leaves, hope soon follows after.[107]

## AN EXISTENTIAL CRISIS: THE LOSS OF MEANING

Our culture is growing increasingly cynical and skeptical and for good reason. When the major building blocks of culture all seem to be weighed and found wanting, it leaves us with nothing to lean upon, nothing to trust in. When we are unable to trust, we lose hope for the future. The antithesis of hope is despair. We despair when we can no longer find anything on which to lean. Meaning is directly connected to our assumptive world. Jeffrey Kauffman explained,

> The assumptive world concept refers to the assumptions or beliefs that ground, secure, or orient people, that give a sense of reality, meaning, or purpose to life. The assumption may be that I am a good person, that I will grow old with my spouse, that God is just, that others may be trusted, that things are or will be a certain way, that there is a future.[108]

What happened to us on 9-11 is only part of the traumatic loss we have suffered. Life as we knew it, or at least as we assumed it was, seems to be no longer so. Our three fundamental assumptions—the world is benevolent; the world is meaningful; the self is worthy—have all been brought into question in this brave new world in which we find ourselves.[109] It's more than the threat of global terrorism, the fear of global warming, the increasing ineffectiveness of the government, or the reality of a new global economy. It is an existential crisis of meaning.

---

107 Donovan Campbell, *The Leader's Code: Mission, Character, Service, and Getting the Job Done* (New York: Random House, 2013), xiii (italics added).

108 Jeffrey Kauffman, ed., *Loss of the Assumptive World: A Theory of Traumatic Loss* (New York: Brunner-Routledge, 2002), 1.

109 These are the three core assumptions according to Ronnie Janoff-Bulman's shattered assumptions theory.

The loss of this assumptive world has been concurrent with our shift away from a culture of character and to a culture of personality for the last century or so. Could it be that the loss of meaning and the growing sense of skepticism we feel are the end results of our attempt to live lives devoid of this foundational quality of character? Philosophers for centuries have connected the good life with the life of high moral character. We have most recently tried to disconnect the two.

Character, as Campbell pointed out, is the foundation of trust. Healthy teams are built on trust and therefore built on the requisite character that underlies it. How then do we define this all-important trait we call character?

## WHAT IS CHARACTER?

It can be argued that much of the organizational dysfunction we experience can be traced back to character problems. Frequently, a thorough incident review reveals the existence of significant character deficits that have contributed to the development and maintenance of organizational difficulties. Character seems to be the foundation of organizational health. Its absence seems to underlie a lack thereof. But what is character itself?

Several commonly quoted concepts begin to define the contours of character. Some have said that character is who you are and what you do when no one else is looking. Others have suggested that character is a consistency between what you say you will do and what you actually do. John Wooden, famously quoting Dale Carnegie, said, "Be more concerned with your character than your reputation, because your character is what you really are, while your reputation is merely what others think you are."[110]

Character is synonymous with our highest human aspirations. To possess character is a noble personal goal. Stephen R. Covey defined character as related to habits:

> Our character, BASICALLY, is a composite of our habits. "Sow a thought, reap an action; sow an action, reap a habit; sow a habit, reap a character; sow a character, reap a destiny," the maxim goes. Habits are powerful forces in our lives. Because they are consistent, often unconscious patterns, they constantly, daily express our character.[111]

If Covey is right, habits can be in thought or action, cognitive or behavioral. But can habits also be emotional? Can we develop an emotional habit of responding in certain ways to certain stimuli? If so, can we alter our emotional responses in the same way we change our thinking or behavior? Our character is actually a composite of being (thinking and emoting) and doing. Character, as defined in the remainder of this volume, is a broad category that refers to our moral and emotional fabric.

### Character = Ethics (doing the right thing) + EQ (being emotionally mature)

While attempting to organize a subject as complex as character, let it be understood from the outset that there are significant overlaps in the categories with which we discuss character. It seems to be inevitably so. Nevertheless, in the midst of an imperfect attempt to develop an imperfect model of character, I

110 Dale Carnegie, *How to Win Friends and Influence People*, (New York: Simon & Schuster, 1936).

111 Stephen R. Covey, *The Seven Habits of Highly Effective People: Powerful Lessons in Personal Change* (New York: Fireside, 1989), 46.

hope to touch on most of the critical components. Let's begin with the ethical side of character.

## ETHICAL LIVING

These ethical traits will not show up on a résumé. They can't necessarily be measured with an assessment. They are evidenced in real life situations that individuals of moral excellence successfully navigate along their journey. Sometimes we are able to obtain character witnesses that will testify to the reality of these qualities observed in someone.

Whereas emotional intelligence refers to a way of being, ethics touches what we do, how we conduct ourselves in the real world. A statement perhaps erroneously attributed to Edmund Burke informs this discussion. He is purported by some to have said, "The only thing necessary for evil to prevail in the world is for good men to do nothing." Thomas Jefferson said similarly, "All tyranny needs to gain a foothold is for people of good conscience to remain silent."

My beautiful wife innocently, yet profoundly, pointed out the logical fallacy in the above statements. She asked me, "If someone does nothing, doesn't that mean that they aren't a 'good' person in the first place?" For her and for most of us, someone's goodness is determined by their right actions. Not acting in the face of impending evil or tyranny, remaining silent and doing nothing, is representative of the unethical disposition of the individual. What then describes the way ethical people behave? The following ethical categories are offered as a partial answer:

# HONESTY

Honesty is truthfulness. Truth is the very foundation of a just society. Without truth, the moral fabric and the perpetuity of a culture cannot be sustained. So it is with an organization. Organizations cannot sustain a cultural foundation characterized by dishonesty. Truth is the bedrock on which shared character, the foundation of the company, rests. Therefore, honesty begins the description of the ethics of character that characterizes healthy teams.

Honest people are honest first with themselves. Honesty with self opens up the possibility for honest dealings with others. When we are dishonest with ourselves, we find ourselves trapped in a web of self-deception and defenses that doesn't allow us to step toward the freedom that comes with real honesty. Honesty is simply telling the truth, saying that which corresponds with reality to the best of our knowledge and ability. Are our teams characterized by honesty?

# INTEGRITY

Personal integrity and its various synonyms or related terms (wholeness, congruence, transparency, authenticity) are buzzwords today. We may not be sure what is wrong in our society, but it seems somehow related to a lack of people being the "real deal." All of these interrelated concepts describe someone being whole or undivided. There is an internal connection of all aspects of their lives. They are integrated. There is no duplicity, no double life, no glaring incongruities. This is integrity.

This crisis of integrity often begins at the top with leaders. When a significant gap exists between their aspirational or professed values and actual practices, they fuel significant disillusionment and disengagement on the team. To ask others to do something

they are unwilling to do is to play the hypocrite. The unsaid
motto of some team members and leaders is often, "Do as I say,
not as I do." People of character do not knowingly play the hypocrite in this way. Stephen M. R. Covey defined integrity:

> To many, "integrity" basically means "honesty." While integrity in-
> cludes honesty, it's much more. It's integratedness. It's walking your
> talk. It's being congruent, inside and out. It's having the courage to
> act in accordance with your values and beliefs.[112]

Character is first an individual trait present in each member of
the team, and only then can it be enjoyed as part of the shared
culture. Personal integrity is personal. People of integrity have
"the courage to change themselves; they model the behavior
they are asking of others." Quinn added, this "personal change is
the way to avoid slow death."[113]

Many of these ethical traits can be further clarified by discussing
their opposite principle. The exact opposite of integrity is well-
summed up in the term hypocrisy. To play the hypocrite is to be
guilty of wearing a mask, of pretending to be something and
someone the person is not. The mask of professed aspirational
values hides the reality of actual and practiced values. To move
toward integrity and wholeness is to move away from hypocrisy
and duplicitousness. Healthy teams are not stages on which to
perform. They create safety, the ability to remove the mask and
be our true selves with one another.

## PERSONAL ACCOUNTABILITY

People who are dishonest with themselves and lack integrity
are prone to placing blame onto others. John Miller identified

---

112 Stephen M. R. Covey, *The Speed of Trust: The One Thing That Changes Everything*
(New York: Free Press, 2006), 54.

113 Quinn, *Deep Change*, 35.

that this lack of personal accountability is revealed in the kinds of questions we ask, whether spoken or part of our internal dialogue. We tend to ask who, when, and why questions that inevitably lead us to place blame and personal responsibility on others. Instead, Miller contended, we need to be asking the questions behind the questions.[114]

Observe how Donovan Campbell, a former Marine, described the application of personal accountability to our lives:

> We can start by identifying those people who tell us hard truths about ourselves. We need to find *people who are not afraid to tell us things we do not want to hear because they have a genuine desire to make us better.* . . . It feels much better to ignore or explain away our weaknesses. In some cases, we may well accept feedback, but only in certain "safe" categories. . . . *The areas where we need the most exposure are often the ones we most want to keep hidden.* We are worried about what will happen if other people get to know the real us.[115]

Deep change, as Robert Quinn aptly described it is a terrifying experience. He called it, "walking naked into the land of uncertainty." The most difficult aspect of deep change is this area of personal accountability. Quinn continued,

> When we see the need for deep change, we usually see it as something that needs to take place in someone else. . . . One of the most important insights about the need to bring about deep change in others has to do with where deep change actually starts. . . . Each of us has the potential to change the world. Because the price of deep change is so high, we seldom take on the challenge. . . . That price [*of not pursuing deep change*] is the choice of slow death, a meaningless and frustrating experience enmeshed in fear, anger, and helplessness, while moving surely toward what is most feared.[116]

---

114 See John Miller, *QBQ, The Question Behind the Question: What to Really Ask Yourself to Eliminate Blame, Victim Thinking, Complaining, and Procrastination.*

115 Campbell, *Leader's Code*, 218 (italics added).

116 Quinn, *Deep Change*, 11 (italics added).

## IMPARTIALITY

Not only are people of character honest, congruent, and personally accountable, they also seek to remain impartial. To be impartial is not the same as to be neutral. People of ethical character are not Switzerland. They see things clearly and attempt to judge things equitably, that is, without the intrusion of personal biases and self-interest. The picture of justice personified is a woman blindfolded holding the scales. She is blind to biases and weighs the scales of objective truth.

Impartiality is a part of our ethical character that keeps us from the less-than-ethical "isms" that often destroy the moral fabric of the team. Three of the big ones are individualism, favoritism, and nepotism. Impartiality resists the urge to simply feather one's own nest, to be ruled by self-serving bias and self-interest. People of higher ethical standards pursue ever-increasing levels of objectivity and freedom from bias as they seek to make judgments that are in the best interest, not simply of themselves, but of the team as a whole.

## HUMILITY

This quality is related to both honesty, being truthful with oneself and others about oneself, and the emotional intelligence trait of self-awareness.

**People of character lead from a place of humility, recognizing their lack and being honest about it.**

This is a vulnerable place to lead from. Though we strive for greater integrity, we never fully arrive. The leader at all levels of the organization is fully aware of this reality. He or she builds integrity in a far different way than those who wear the mask of pretended authenticity.

The vulnerable person of influence sees the remaining gaps between aspirational values and practiced values. This is a key, not only to remaining humble, but to effectiveness in leading and serving others. Quinn commented, "The heart of effectiveness . . . is building integrity through the constant observation of one's lack of integrity." [117] Here is the irony, being mindful of the gap is not a disqualification from leadership; it is a character-based prerequisite. Humble leaders are servant–leaders who do not abuse the power given to them for the good of others. As Abraham Lincoln is attributed to have said, "Nearly all men can stand adversity, but if you want to test a man's character, give him power."

## COURAGE

Courage is a word that has fallen from frequent use in our modern language. It hearkens back to days gone by and reminds us of greater generations that preceded us. Courage can be divided into two types. "Physical courage," said Donovan Campbell, "[is] risking life and limb in pursuit of a worthy mission." It is the bravery of war and is universally respected in our culture. Campbell discussed another type of courage, *moral courage*, described as follows:

> This courage does not risk lives; rather it risks livelihoods. It does not push through physical pain, but it does accept emotional trauma. It may not incur bodily harm, but it may require difficult, even life-altering decisions to be made in a matter of seconds. Put simply, moral courage is that form of courage that overcomes fear to speak the truth to power, even—and especially—when power doesn't want to hear the truth. In so doing, the morally courageous

117 Quinn, Deep Change, 76.

put their positions, their reputations, and their abilities to provide for their families on the line.[118]

Moral courage overcomes one of the most powerful and basic human drives, self-preservation. It is the character trait that allows the courageous to do the right thing even at great personal cost. It is an inner strength that perseveres despite peer pressure, societal expectation, and groupthink.

Moral courage is the opposite of willful blindness. People with willful blindness, out of fear of retaliation and not wanting to be identified as whistle-blowers, refuse to see things as they are. People with moral courage do the right thing, knowing the potential personal price they are likely to pay. Joe Darby, the soldier who found the photos at Abu Ghraib and decided to turn them in, knew the price he would probably pay from his fellow soldiers who were pictured in them. Nonetheless, he chose to take the morally courageous course and stand up for his core belief in basic human dignity, even that of his Iraqi enemies imprisoned there.

There is another, a third, form of courage. This courage is directly linked to the concept of personal vulnerability. Brené Brown suggested that "vulnerability is the most accurate measurement of courage."[119] In our society, we have an undiscerned contradiction regarding vulnerability. On one hand, we tend to think of it as a weakness. On the other, when we see the huge risk on the part of the truly vulnerable, we are forced to acknowledge it as a

---

118 Campbell, *Leader's Code*, 137.

119 Brené Brown, "Listening to Shame," TEDtalk, March 2012, accessed October 21, 2013, http:// www.ted.com/talks/brene_brown_listening_to_shame.html.

strength. To be vulnerable is to risk the shame of rejection. Those who truly lead face this fear and press forward with courage.

**Courage consists of three types: physical courage, moral courage, and the courage to be vulnerable.**

## LOYALTY

*Semper fi.* The US Marines understand this attribute of character. Marines are "always faithful (loyal)." *Fi* is the Latin for faithful. From this same root, we derive the word "fidelity" or speak of a "fiduciary" responsibility. Fidelity is a sense of loyalty to country, cause, and one another. Loyalty is a disappearing commodity in 2013 America.

Loyalty is nonneutrality. If I am a fan of the Los Angeles Dodgers (my local team while growing up), I am loyal to my team. Accordingly, I am not a fan of the San Francisco Giants. The deeper the rivalry, the deeper the loyalty. If I root for the Rams, I instinctively root against the Forty-Niners. If for the Lakers, then not for the Celtics. Neutrality is nonloyalty or indifference.

Loyalty underlies many of the traits above. Loyalty is an other-oriented pursuit, which explains why it may be in such short supply. In a *me* culture, where looking out for number one is the highest value, there is little room for this archaic and cumbersome thing called loyalty. Loyalty often demands a price. Our loyalty to others and to a cause often calls us to suffer personal loss. Zig Ziglar included this trait as a key component of character. "The foundation stones for a balanced success are honesty, character, integrity, faith, love, and *loyalty.*"[120]

---

120 Zig Ziglar, The Ziglar Way, accessed November 8, 2013 (italics added).

## TRUSTWORTHINESS

The qualities discussed above combine to create a person's ethical character. As we will see in the next chapter, trust is a key to healthy team development (cohesiveness) and superior results. The character qualities of honesty, integrity, personal accountability, impartiality, humility, courage, and loyalty combine to create the foundation of trust (trustworthiness). Trust is not freely given; it is earned.

**Ethical Living = Trustworthiness (Honesty + Integrity + Accountability + Impartiality + Humility + Courage + Loyalty)**

## EMOTIONAL INTELLIGENCE

Emotional intelligence is a trait developed over time and usually in response to adversity. The heat of life situations either produces character in various forms, including emotional intelligence, or causes us to regress toward immaturity. It may surprise you to hear of emotional intelligence referred to as a subcategory of character. It surprised me the first time I stumbled onto the connection.

The heart of the assessment model that we utilize in coaching clients is identified as emotional intelligence.[121] It is deeper than our behavioral style, our drives or motivations, our skills or abilities. In the model, it is the heart of who we really are. It is for this reason Daniel Goleman stated that "for leaders, emotional intelligence is almost 90 percent of what sets stars apart from the mediocre."[122] If EQ is the heart of who we are in Goleman's

---

121 For an introduction to the concept of emotional intelligence, see appendix C.

122 Daniel Goleman, *Working with Emotional Intelligence* (New York: Bantam, 1998), back cover.

model, then perhaps it is related to what we formerly considered to be the heart of an individual (character). As I reflected on this potential, it all became quite clear. Emotional intelligence is quite similar to other terms like character, maturity, or adult behavior.[123]

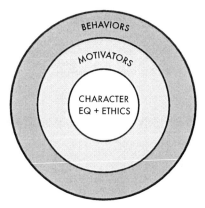

**Figure 13.** Character: the heart of the individual.

Emotional intelligence (in combination with our ethical character) is at the heart of who we are as an individual. Teaching the assessment model with EQ at the center, I began to see how the five traits of emotional intelligence closely correlate to commonly discussed aspects of character or maturity. As related to character development then, consider the five components of emotional intelligence listed below. The fivefold model is comprised of two halves building on one another hierarchally. Emotional intelligence begins with intrapersonal traits.

## INTRAPERSONAL EQ

Intrapersonal emotional intelligence refers to those aspects that are within the individual and in reference to the self. This is con-

---

123 It is the nature of a child to be emotionally immature. How often do we observe biological adults in their seventies resembling emotional teenagers? This seems to be a character or maturity problem. They never fullly grew up.

nected to the ancient wisdom, "Know thyself." It begins with the trait of self-awareness.

## Self-Awareness (Humility)

Daniel Goleman defined self-awareness as "an ongoing attention to one's internal states." He continued to describe this state in which the "mind observes and investigates experience itself, including the emotions."[124] True self-awareness leads to humility, "a realistic and unflinching view of yourself and your relationships." Donovan Campbell continued, "By gaining a deeper and more realistic knowledge of ourselves, we become more humble."[125]

## Self-Regulation (Self-Control)

A necessary addition to self-awareness of an internal emotional state is the trait of self-regulation. Being able to self-regulate, to bring oneself more quickly back to a calm, nonemotionally charged place, is a learned skill that is part of overall emotional intelligence. People who are unable to control their emotional state and the resulting behavior are often seen as having a character problem. Mature adults are able to successfully manage their own emotional state in such a way that they do not become emotionally hijacked, doing or saying things they later regret.

## Motivation (Diligence)

Human beings who are immature (undeveloped in the skill of motivation) will give up and throw in the towel as part of an emotionally overwhelmed experience. Learning to persist and

---

124 Daniel Goleman, *Emotional Intelligence: Why It Can Matter More Than IQ* (New York: Bantam Books, 1995), 46.

125 Campbell, *Leader's Code*, 39.

to control our emotions, to keep going even when it is difficult, is a critical part of our character. Helen Keller said it well,

> Character cannot be developed in ease and quiet. Only through experience of trial and suffering can the soul be strengthened, ambition inspired, and success achieved.[126]

## INTERPERSONAL EQ

Interpersonal emotional intelligence refers to those skills and abilities, levels of maturity or character, that are at work in an individual as he or she relates and interacts with others.

### Empathy

Interestingly, empathy is a key component to our emotional intelligence and the one most notably lacking among individuals who exhibit narcissistic or entitled personalities. Empathy for others is a huge prevention of the potential damage to others from overly entitled individuals (according to the Demand Model of conflict). Empathy, deep compassion for others and the ability to walk in their shoes, is most definitely the possession of mature human beings.

### Social Skills (Attunement)

Putting all these skills together to successfully manage oneself and one's relational world is reliant on the skill called attunement. Attunement, according to Daniel Pink, is

> the ability to bring one's actions and outlook into harmony with other people and with the context you're in.[127]

This is the use of emotional intelligence to align successfully with others around you and to meaningfully connect with them.

---

126 Helen Keller, *The Story of My Life*, (New York, 1903).

127 Daniel Pink, *To Sell Is Human: The Surprising Truth about Moving Others* (New York: Penguin, 2012), 70.

**Emotional Intelligence (EQ) =**
**Self-Awareness (Humility) + Emotional Regulation (Self-**
**Control) + Motivation (Diligence) + Empathy +**
**Social Skills (Attunement to Others)**

# CHARACTER

Putting both halves of EQ and ethical living together, we can see the whole definition of character, the shared foundation of healthy teams. Trustworthiness, the requisite relational character displayed in the past to allow ourselves to be trusted by others in the future, is closely identified with character. Campbell defined character as

> an honorable individual condition gained through the intentional pursuit of virtue and maintained over the course of a lifetime. . . . The various military branches express the virtues underpinning character in different ways, but in all of their forms they can be boiled down to the following six: (1) Humility, (2) Excellence, (3) Kindness, (4) Discipline, (5) Courage, (6) Wisdom.[128]

Notice how Donovan Campbell's definition weaves in both sides of our proposed model: EQ and ethical living. When we look at the traits we have discussed, we can see how these traits work together to form the core of the individual that we identify as character. Character is reflected in our being and in our doing.

---

128 Campbell, *Leader's Code*, xxiii.

**Table 7.** The Two Sides of Character

| CHARACTER | |
| --- | --- |
| **ETHICS** | **EMOTIONAL INTELLIGENCE** |
| *Doing* | *Being* |
| Honesty | Self-Awareness (Humility) |
| Integrity / Accountability | Self-Regulation (Self-Control) |
| Impartiality | Motivation (Diligence) |
| Courage | Empathy (Compassion) |
| Loyalty | Social Skills (Attunement) |
| **TRUSTWORTHINESS (CREDIBILITY)** | |

# TRUSTWORTHINESS (CREDIBILITY)

Stephen M. R. Covey defined credibility as the combination of character (integrity and intent) and competence (capabilities and results). This definition is very similar to our concept of character. Trustworthiness, the quality of proving trustable in the past, and credibility, the quality that results from a history of being credible, are the result of character exercised over time.

Character, shared and practiced among the members and particularly by team leaders, is the foundation of healthy, productive, and successful teams. This contrasts with the myth of the charismatic leader. Collins and Porras unequivocally stated that "a high-profile, charismatic style is absolutely not required to successfully shape a visionary company."[129] This is further evidence that we are beginning to recover from the myth of the charismatic leader inherited from Dale Carnegie and others from the early 1900s to the present. Similarly, the Level 5 Leaders discovered by Jim Collins in *Good to Great* were "known not for

---

129 Jim Collins and Jerry Porras, *Built to Last: Successful Habits of Visionary Companies* (New York: Penguin Group, 2009), 32.

their flash or charisma but for extreme humility coupled with intense professional will." Collin's lesson as summed up by Susan Cain is clear. "We don't need giant personalities to transform companies. We need leaders who build not their own egos [*I'm great*] but the institutions they run."[130]

## BUILDING A CULTURE OF CHARACTER

Character begins as an individual pursuit and discipline. No one else can make us people of character. We must recognize, however, the impact of the systems in which we live. In cultures of high character, the individual team member's pursuit of this trait is encouraged, motivated, and strengthened as each member and the team as a whole jointly pursue this end. As we each work toward greater individual character, holding each other accountable for the way we live with one another in the workplace, we form a powerful trait called shared character.

**Shared character is a sort of positive peer pressure, a cultural creation that makes it easier to do the right thing than to compromise shared values and morals.**

Shared character serves as a foundation to a healthy team.[131] It is an essential starting point and a place to return to when the team is unsure where to go. For this reason, character is the building block that supports the team dynamics of cohesion and clarity.

---

130 Cain, *Quiet*, 54–55 (italics added).

131 Among the traits of potential client disqualification is this aspect of character. Unethical leaders can never create an environment of organizational or team health.

# 9

# STRONG COHESIVENESS

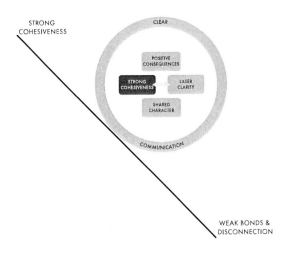

## COHESIVENESS

Cohesiveness is the glue that holds the team together. Many of the concepts that are used to describe healthy teams have a degree of overlap. When we speak of cohesion, bonding, or attachment, we approach the terrain of emotional intelligence. To put it plainly, cohesiveness is an aftereffect of emotional intelligence, a component of character. Emotional intelligence, awareness of self and attunement to others, creates the bond. Daniel Goleman stated it plainly:

Managing emotions is how you build a team, an organization. It's the ability to get team members inspired. It's about dealing with emotions, building high emotions, and creating an inspired team. If you've ever been in a high-performing team, it just inspires, even though there is stress and challenge. And there's always going to be a leader, as part of that process, to build creativity. So it's essential for leaders to understand how team bonding works and how bonding in a team will build energy.[132]

Character, specifically emotional intelligence, aids in bonding or cohesion. Less-than-excellent teams often experience a lack of attachment, a sense of disconnection from one another and often from the mission. This is due, in part, to the type of glue we use to bond the team together.

## TWO TYPES OF GLUE

Team cohesiveness is about bonding, being connected to one another. Cohesiveness is a part of the culture of the tribe that hopefully includes higher levels of character, the combination of ethics and emotional intelligence. Sadly, this is not always the case. Many teams experience an inferior form of cohesion based on the glue of fear.

Fear is a motivator. Machiavelli, based on his low view of human beings as essentially selfish and lazy, advocated for the use of fear as the primary means of motivation. This culture of fear has dominated the landscape of the workplace, the family, and other social groups for centuries. In a fear-based corporate culture, the focus is on survival. All available energy is expended

---

132 Daniel Goleman, "Bonding creates high-performing teams," LinkedIn post, accessed June 5, 2013, http://www.linkedin.com/today/post/article/20130305194109 -117825785-bonding-creates-high -performing-teams?trk=mp-author-card.

trying to simply make it. This survival-based culture creates inferior but, nonetheless, real bonds.

Groups motivated by fear huddle together as a protective in-
stinct. Leaders that set the tone for organizational culture often
use fear as their primary method of control. Fear works fairly
well in the short term and with repetitive and noncreative tasks,
neither of which is very common today in the American workplace. Like a herd of antelope on the African plains, the group
draws together as a way of seeking strength in numbers or even
getting lost in the crowd, unseen by the fear-based predatory
leader. This cohesion the group experiences is externally driven
and involuntary. The external threat of the boss or other leaders
or strong personalities drives this culture of fear and intimida-
tion. The group is bonded but not in a healthy way that will lead
to positive consequences.

### Groups that are motivated by trust are entirely different than groups connected by fear.

They still draw together or bond but for very different reasons. In
a culture of trust, leaders inspire others to draw closer through
creating an environment of safety and vulnerability. Here again,
tribal leaders set the tone for the followers. Trust bonds are
choice based rather than forced. They are internally driven and
voluntary. They are not created out of compulsion or necessity.
The group chooses to draw together based on mutual care,
trust, and respect. This kind of cohesiveness is only possible as
teams move closer to stage 4 or stage 5 tribal principles. As you
can see next, these two bonds are quite different and produce
quite different results.

**Table 8.** Two Types of Bonding

| Culture of Fear | CULTURAL DIVIDE | Culture of Trust |
|---|---|---|
| Shame | | Vulnerability |
| Hiding | | Openness |
| Defending (Protecting) | | Ownership |
| Blaming | | Honesty |
| ↓ | | ↓ |
| **Inferior Bonds** | | **Superior Bonds** |

The glue we use to bond the team matters deeply. What follows is a description of the various facets of a trust-based culture of cohesion. Extraordinarily healthy teams are highly bonded as a unit through the ongoing cultivation of the following traits.

## MUTUAL ACCOUNTABILITY

Personal accountability was discussed in the previous chapter as an aspect of personal character. Shared or mutual account-ability is the group maintenance and encouragement of per-sonal accountability among each of the team members. Healthy teams hold one another accountable. This is a form of positive peer pressure. In fact, it is mutual accountability—not hierarchal accountability—that is most effective in healthy organizations. As Patrick Lencioni pointed out,

> Peer-to-peer accountability is the primary and most effective source of accountability on the leadership team of a healthy or-ganization. Most people assume that the leader of an executive team should be the primary source of accountability—and that's the norm in most unhealthy organizations—but it isn't efficient or practical, and it makes little sense.[133]

---

133 Lencioni, *The Advantage*, 54.

Mutual accountability is not micromanaging. Micromanaging is based fundamentally on distrust. "I don't trust you to be personally accountable, so I feel compelled to manage you." This is not the case among healthy teams that are bonded together with strong cords of trust.

## TRUST

Trust is the air that healthy relationships breathe. Without trust, relationship is a misnomer. Supposed relationships that are based on mutual distrust and suspicion are not relationships at all. Stephen M. R. Covey said it well:

> There is one thing that is common to every individual, relationship, team, family, organization, nation, economy, and civilization throughout the world—one thing which, if removed, will destroy the most powerful government, the most successful business, the most thriving economy, the most influential leadership, the greatest friendship, the strongest character, the deepest love.[134]

That one thing is trust. And yet, we are currently in the midst of a crisis of trust in America. We no longer trust our government, our corporations, our religious institutions, our families. None of these is without good warrant. Unfortunately, many have experienced disappointment and disillusionment with all of these societal institutions and have found themselves in a culture that is cynical, skeptical, and fundamentally distrusting. When we seek to build trust as a foundational aspect of healthy team cohesion, we are most definitely working counter culturally, or uphill.

Built on a foundation of shared character that reflects trustworthiness, healthy teams have a significant advantage related to

---

134 Covey, *Speed of Trust*, 1.

the presence of deep mutual trust. Trust can be defined as confidence. When we trust others, we believe that they truly have our best interest at heart. When we live in a trust-based environment, we are able to lower defenses and accomplish better results by focusing our energy on the task at hand versus self-protection. Trust's opposite is suspicion. Teams with low levels of trust expend significant energy managing all the signs that indicate a lack of safety. Suspicion is not only emotionally exhausting to the individuals on the team, it greatly reduces all aspects of team member performance including engagement, creativity, and flow.

## THE BETRAYAL OF DISENGAGEMENT

Trust is normally built in small, seemingly insignificant moments and ways. It is built every time we choose to move toward rather than away from another person, when we choose to respond to their bids for relationship rather than ignore them. There are various destroyers of trust in teams and relationships. The more obvious ones usually involve various overt forms of betrayal: a coworker or boss uses vulnerabilities shared in confidence against someone. In that moment, trust is almost completely obliterated. There is, however, a more subtle and insidious form of betrayal that destroys trust equally as well. Brené Brown described it.

> This betrayal usually happens long before the other ones. I'm talking about *the betrayal of disengagement*. Of not caring. Of letting the connection go. Of not being willing to devote time and effort to the relationship. . . . When the people we love [*or work with*] or with whom we have a deep connection stop caring, stop paying attention, stop investing, and stop fighting for the relationship, trust begins to slip away and hurt starts seeping in. Disengagement triggers shame and our greatest fears—the fears of being abandoned, unworthy, and unlovable.[135]

---

135 Brown, *Daring Greatly*, 51–52 (italics added).

This pulling away kills trust. The opposite of love is not hate, not the practice of covert acts of aggression or betrayal, but rather indifference. The betrayal of disengagement is a form of practiced indifference, communicating to our opponents on the team that they don't even matter.

There is another similar form of betrayal that also erodes the development of trust. Sometimes, a previously valued member of a team begins to be systematically devalued by the team. Those traits that were once appreciated and admired are now viewed in a negative light. One common tactic employed in a less-than-healthy team culture is to simply move away from the individual who doesn't "fit" any longer. The individual experiences a systematic devaluation over time that Bill Bonstetter called the Zero Cycle:

> It is the gradual destruction of who you are, your Real Self. When you are operating in an environment that does not value you— an environment that discourages or hinders your personal growth and development, you will experience low self-esteem, which leads to low self-efficacy. . . . The continual battering of your self-esteem gradually wears you down. You are not designed to be devalued.[136]

Mattering and trusting go together. When we are devalued and abandoned, our ability to trust is correspondingly destroyed.

Deepening trust opens the door to increased vulnerability, honesty, and creativity. Healthy teams prize trust as the chief measure of their cohesion. The only thing that may prove more useful to developing cohesive teams is vulnerability, which is the direct corollary of trust.

---

136 Bonstetter, *If I Only Knew,* 29–30.

# VULNERABILITY

Ironically, trust is built on and produces vulnerability. It's a chicken-and-egg concept. Vulnerability, instead of being a weakness as is commonly believed, is actually a strength. We have been conditioned to think of vulnerability as a liability; when we see it in others, however, it is clearly an asset. When leaders make themselves vulnerable, it increases our connection to them. When team members push through the barrier of shame to greater vulnerability, trust is heightened, and cohesiveness is increased.

**Vulnerability breeds higher levels of trust in the team.**

Great teams understand these principles. They know firsthand the power of setting aside the masks that protect them from the gaze of others. In an atmosphere of trust, we are encouraged to risk being vulnerable. Vulnerable teams are trusting teams and vice versa.

Vulnerability can only occur in environments that are safe enough. When we perceive a lack of personal safety, we instinctively withdraw like a turtle into its shell. Safety is created and reinforced every day as we interact within our team culture. As with many other aspects of team health, it starts at the top. The leaders in the organization or the team set the tone of being safe individuals and creating a safe culture. When tribal culture is safe enough and vulnerability is modeled and protected by the tribe, an amazing thing happens. They can begin to passionately disagree.

# RIGOROUS DEBATE

Many teams operate under the illusion that unanimous deci-sions are an indication of healthy unified teams. There is an un-healthy form of unanimity, however, that arises from the fear of potential conflict that may be triggered by suggesting alternate thoughts or opinions. In these teams, silence and overagree-ment are characteristic. They don't engage in rigorous ideologi-cal debate ever for fear of the destruction they see as intrinsi-cally connected to debate or disagreement. The discomfort of discussing differing and competing ideas is too great to risk breaking the perceived unity. Margaret Heffernan described this phenomenon well:

> If one of the symptoms of blindness is comfort, so one of the in-dicators of critical thinking may be discomfort. That's why unani-mous decisions are intrinsically suspicious. Were there no options? No alternatives? *Unanimous decisions are incomplete decisions, made when there was too much power in the room, too much obedi-ence, and too much conformity.* If only one solution is visible, look again.[137]

To "look again," we need to overcome our collective fear. Daniel Goleman aptly proposed that "open discussion and disagree-ments about ideas—as opposed to attacks on people who hold disparate views—sharpen decision making." Instead, such teams quietly adopt a habit of "avoiding all disputes."[138] This culture of fear is not conducive to increased creativity or greater results. Fear has a way of killing team spirit and effectiveness.

There is no clear consensus regarding the goodness or badness of conflict in an organization. We, as a society, are not sure what

---

137 Heffernan, *Willful Blindness*, 239 (italics added).

138 Daniel Goleman, *Primal Leadership: Realizing the Power of Emotional Intelligence* (Boston: Harvard Business School Publishing, 2002), 172.

we think about conflict. Though the undeniable negative con-notation of conflict proper was demonstrated in Part 1, many continue to try to see conflict as a good thing. Patrick Lencioni, for example, saw conflict as existing along a continuum from "artificial harmony" to "mean-spirited personal attacks" with the sweet spot being in the middle where constructive and destructive conflict meet. Healthy teams, according to Lencioni, have "constructive conflict."[139] The heart of his point is well taken. Constructive conflict, however, may be a bit of an oxymoron. Conflict can and should be differentiated from disagreement and debate. It is helpful to distinguish for the sake of team clarity between these related, yet dissimilar, terms. Here, the healthy group dynamic is intentionally labeled as rigorous debate, healthy disagreement (Agreeing to disagree is contrary to healthy disagreement.), or respectful and honest discussion.

Conflict, according to our emotions driven by our limbic system, is a bad thing. If it were a good thing, we would not feel such instinctive fear. It is fear of conflict and the relational fallout that hinders many teams from engaging in healthy debate, discussion, or disagreement. When teams do not engage in rigorous debate, they opt for a far less creative interaction that is driven by groupthink. Irving Janis described this dynamic:

> Each individual in the group feels himself to be under an injunction to avoid making penetrating criticisms that might bring on a clash with fellow members and destroy the unity of the group. . . . Each member avoids interfering with the emerging consensus by assuring himself that the opposing arguments he had in mind must be erroneous or that his misgivings are too unimportant to be worth mentioning.[140]

---

139 Lencioni, *The Advantage*, 42.
140 Irving Janis quoted in Goleman, *Vital Lies*, 181.

Each member of the group personally censors for the sake of preserving the illusion of one big happy family. Goleman continued to describe the outworking of groupthink among the team.

> Instead of hiding a secret or shared distress, the group simply cramps its attention and hobbles its information-seeking to preserve a cozy unanimity. Loyalty to the group requires that members not raise embarrassing questions, attack weak arguments, or counter softheaded thinking with hard facts. Only comfortable shared schemas are allowed full expression.[141]

Disagreement is not conflict.

**Disagreement is, in fact, a sign of team health.**

Healthy teams engage in rigorous and respectful debate because they have previously cultivated a strong culture of trust and vulnerability. They don't fear the repercussion of sharing differing thoughts that groups bonded through fear experience far too frequently. There may not be such a thing as constructive conflict, but there is most definitely the practice of rigorous, passionate, and constructive disagreement among healthy teams. In these systems, the shared foundation of character creates a safe-enough environment for everyone on the team to participate.

## FULL PARTICIPATION

Where trust and vulnerability are in short supply, there is little true participation from team members. Instead, there tends to be an unhealthy culture of groupthink driven by fear. Healthy teams that accomplish great things together have higher levels of engagement. Every member of the team feels empowered to fully participate in group discussions, free from the fear of being

141 Ibid., 183.

shamed or embarrassed. Once they have fully contributed to the discussion, they are more able to fully support the decision of the team, even if it differs significantly from their personal proposal.

Healthy teams speak with one voice. When the team has heard honestly from all the members, the group makes a decision that is deemed best. In healthy teams, the group decision is owned by the whole group and by each member. Dissension or disagreement does not linger after group decisions have been made. There aren't private meetings after meetings in the parking lot or the restroom. Team members who feel fully heard and respected are able, with sufficient levels of trust, to release their personal thoughts or ideas and to fully embrace the decision of the whole. When we, as team members, walk out of the room, we own the decision jointly. The decision is *ours*, not *theirs*.[142]

## SHARED OWNERSHIP

Ownership is a key aspect of healthy teams and the capstone of team cohesiveness. We are bonded and unified in our group decisions and strategies.

**Ownership moves *me* to *we* and *them* to *us*.**

As mentioned, great teams that have developed more mature tribal culture do not live in the "I'm great" world. Instead, they live in no less than "we're great" and "our decision and direction are great."

Healthy teams build cultures of trust and vulnerability that are safe enough to encourage rigorous debate, full participation,

---

142 This is indicative of at least stage 4 tribal culture, "we're great."

and shared ownership. The team becomes unified (not uniform) in the midst of a rich diversity of thoughts, opinions, ideas, and experiences. The bonds are not built on fear or groupthink, but rather on deep trust and a genuine desire to fully connect with others from the heart. Cohesive teams are healthy teams.

Our cohesion is first and foremost to one another as people. Reinforcing that bond is the shared connection that we have to the ideals and core values and beliefs that we have established as a team. Ownership is directly related to and built upon the healthy development of team mission, the *why* we exist. As we'll see in the next chapter, cohesion and clarity are essentially cocreated in a reciprocal relationship. The greater we bond, the clearer we share in the commonness of purpose, values, strategy, and direction. The inverse is also true. The clearer we are in regard to both individual and group mission and values, the more we are able to experience ever-deepening bonds of cohesion.

# 10

## LASER CLARITY

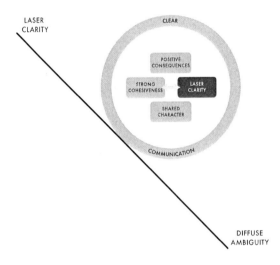

## THE NEED FOR CLARITY

Without clarity, an organization suffers. Without clarity, individuals lack confidence and focus. Where there is no clarity, there is confusion, hesitation, and a host of other company and personal ills. Laser light is intensely focused, not diffused. It provides light and heat on a precise point in space and is nonambiguous. Ambiguity is a team-killing principle. Everything around us is trying to steal clarity. It is noise, static. Great teams move toward ever-increasing levels of both group and individual clarity with laser-like precision.

Sometimes we shed light onto critical areas of the team (mission, purpose, values, culture). Often the light we shed is too weak and too diffuse to provide the level of clarity that healthy teams experience. It cannot be overstated.

**Healthy teams have clarity at both the individual and the group levels that sets them apart from other groups.**

## SHARED (GROUP) CLARITY

Group clarity deals with clear, commonly understood shared responses to the right questions formed using "we." For many years, the Drucker Five (all of which are first-person plural) have been used by organizations to bring collective direction. Recently, Patrick Lencioni suggested six similar questions for use in achieving organizational clarity, a key component of health.[143] Comparing these two sets of questions, we are able to make some interesting observations.

**Table 9.** Key Areas Needing Clarity

|          | **Drucker** | **Lencioni** | **Key Principles of Clarity** |
|----------|-------------|--------------|-------------------------------|
| **IDENTITY** | **What** is our mission? | **Why** do we exist? | Core (Compelling) Shared Purpose |
|          |             | **How** do we behave? | Core Shared Values |
|          | **Who** is our customer? | **What** do we do? | Core Business Definition |

---

143 Lencioni, *The Advantage*, 77.

| | Drucker | Lencioni | Key Principles of Clarity |
|---|---|---|---|
| **STRATEGY** | **What** do they value? | **How** will we succeed? | Core Business Strategy (Market / Client Definition) |
| | **What** are our results? | **What** is most important right now? | Core Short-Term Business Focus |
| | **What** is our plan? | **Who** must do what? | Alignment / Role Clarity |

Teams with laser clarity have deeply held common answers and core convictions concerning these and related questions. Healthy teams invest the requisite time and effort to work as a group until clarity exists in the following areas:

## COMPELLING PURPOSE: WHY DO WE EXIST?

Collins and Porras in *Built to Last* wisely directed us to the centrality of core purpose as the foundational element in visionary companies. They defined core purpose as:

> The organization's *fundamental reason for existence* beyond just making money—a perpetual guiding star on the horizon; not to be confused with specific goals or business strategies.[144]

Having a core purpose (something to believe in) is also an essential ingredient of both Godin and Logan's definitions of tribes. Without a vision, the organization will perish. Lencioni encouraged organizations to define this core purpose in "completely idealistic" terms, to provide a statement that inspires everyone in the organization to accomplish something "grand and inspirational."[145]

---

144 Collins and Porras, *Built to Last,* 73 (italics added).

145 Lencioni, *The Advantage,* 82.

## SINEK'S GOLDEN CIRCLE

In Simon Sinek's best-selling book, *Start with Why*, he proposed that uniquely successful companies and ventures do the opposite of the masses. Instead of starting with *What*, then describing *How*, and ending with *Why* at the periphery, Sinek brilliantly inverted the order of the conversation.

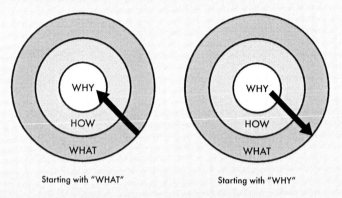

Starting with "WHAT"        Starting with "WHY"

**Figure 14.** The importance of working inside out.

Sinek wisely reminds us of the centrality of vision, the why of the team. The why is the higher purpose to which we aspire. Sinek leaves us with an inspiring challenge as a team:

> Our visions are the world we imagine, the tangible results of what the world would look like if we spent every day in pursuit of our WHY.[146]

Arriving at this compelling purpose for our existence requires persistence and hard work, all the while resisting the temptation to use marketing or business jargon that doesn't help to actually define the shared why. It is hard work to determine our contribution to a better world around us. We are searching as a team for something so inspirational that our shared vision, once

---

146 Simon Sinek, *Start with Why: How Great Leaders Inspire Everyone to Take Action* (New York: Penguin Group, 2009), 228.

we find it, will continue to guide us for many years. When we have clearly defined our reason for existence, our why, we are able to move to the next core ideological question pertaining to our culture: how we are agreeing to behave?

## CORE VALUES (CULTURE): HOW WE BEHAVE

Collins and Porras connected core purpose to core values as together forming the core ideology of the team. They defined core values as

> The organization's essential and enduring tenets—a small set of general guiding principles; not to be confused with specific cultural or operating practices; not to be compromised for financial gain or short-term expediency.[147]

This aspect of organizational clarity closely resembles Logan et al.'s description of tribal culture, the norms that govern tribal living. In the language of *Tribal Leadership*, some tribes are not ready for this discussion. Warren Bennis described this problem as "some tribes [*stage 3 or less*] reject any discussion of values, character, or nobility, while others [*stage 4 or 5*] demand these conversations."[148] For tribes that have matured beyond stage 3, "I'm great," the conversation of values becomes central. In any organization, the discussion of values can be difficult to get started. Nonetheless, this conversation about the elephants in the room is essential to the development of group clarity and consensus.

---

147 Collins and Porras, *Built to Last*, 73.

148 Warren Bennis, as quoted in foreward to Logan, *Tribal Leadership*, xii (italics added).

# BRENÉ BROWN'S TEN QUESTIONS

Brené Brown provided a list of provocative questions aimed at drawing out the reality of practiced culture in an organization.[149] The answers to the following begin to form a picture of culture, "the way we do things around here":

1.  What behaviors are rewarded? Punished?

2.  Where and how are people actually spending their resources (time, money, attention)?

3.  What rules and expectations are followed, enforced, and ignored?

4.  Do people feel safe and supported when talking about how they feel and asking for what they need?

5.  What are the sacred cows? Who is most likely to tip them? Who stands the cows back up?

6.  What stories are legends and what values do they convey?

7.  What happens when someone fails, disappoints, or makes a mistake?

8.  How is vulnerability (uncertainty, risk, and emotional exposure) perceived?

9.  How prevalent are shame and blame and how are they showing up?

10. What's the collective tolerance for discomfort? Is the discomfort of learning, trying new things, and giving and receiving feedback normalized, or is there a high premium put on comfort (and how does that look)?

---

149 Brown, *Daring Greatly*, 174–5.

Brown's questions can help us get started. Using whatever means are at our disposal, our task is to identify the two to three core values that uniquely speak to how we choose to behave culturally. They are our guiding principles around tribal culture, norms, and behavior. They are often related to and built on our shared character, but go deeper and more clearly identify our key cultural principles. Team behavior in accordance with non-negotiable values is a character issue. Core values rise above that foundational conversation.

Our core values already exist at a significant level in and among our teams. To qualify as such, they cannot be things to which we only aspire and do not practice. Since none of us as individuals or teams has arrived, healthy teams recognize the potential for more fully and consistently living out their core values on a daily basis. The potential gap that can develop between the core values we profess on the poster and our actual behavior is a major contributor to disillusionment and disengagement (breakdown of cohesion) on the team. Clarity builds cohesion and vice versa.

## ORGANIZATIONAL FOCUS: WHAT DO WE DO?

Peter Drucker's question "What do we do?" sheds light on the business definition of healthy organizations. Knowing what we do as a business and how our specific team fits into that clarity differentiates healthy teams from others. This question needs to be answered after gaining clarity on our core purpose and values. As Sinek suggested, companies that rise above the rest begin with *why*, move to *how*, and only then begin to get clear about *what*.

What we do is connected to Drucker's questions of "Who is our customer?" and "What do they value?" Our core business or organizational definition will include clarity on *who* we are serving and *what* we are providing to them. It may help us define our core business focus if we spend some time thinking deeply about our primary customers or clients. Who are they? What are we doing or providing for them? Once we are clear, the team needs to finish this process and commit to writing the core definition.

The statement should be simple and to the point in response to, what do you do? It doesn't need to be overly complicated, qualified with adjectives describing how we do what we do, or confused with the core purpose statement. A core business definition is a simple, clear, and straightforward statement of what goods or services the organization provides to whom:

- An optometry practice: *We provide a full-scope of eye care services to everyone in our community.*

- A construction management company: *We provide complete construction management and general contracting services to clients with building needs.*

This is the third key aspect of shared clarity.

## SHARED STRATEGY: HOW WILL WE ACHIEVE OUR GOALS?

Once we are clear on our core purpose, our reason for existence (our why), our core values, our tribal culture (our how), and our core business definition (what we do), only then can we begin to reflect on the question of *how* as it pertains to strategy. This is a different *how* than the how of core values (how we agree to conduct ourselves). It is very similar to the game plan utilized in sporting events. At this point along the path of healthy team development toward laser clarity, we are now ready to begin to define our common shared strategy, our game plan that describes how we intend to bring our *why* into existence.

Strategy is the big-picture plan as to how we collectively see ourselves achieving the success and results we aim to deliver. Like a game plan, it often has to be readjusted continuously throughout the game and perhaps at halftime, as we reflect on the first half and make adjustments for the second. Agreement and commonality around this question are important among the team members so that individuals don't move in opposite directions unintentionally as they think about implementation. Our core strategy informs how we understand the challenge, the primary ways in which we plan to tackle it, and lastly, tells us all what we are not doing. It removes strategy-related options from the table, hopefully avoiding the all-too-present problem of spinning our wheels as a team.

To summarize, group clarity that is laser focused exists at four critical levels, in order of priority as follows:

**Table 10.** Ascending Levels of Group Clarity

| Levels of Clarity | | |
|---|---|---|
| **WHY** | Core Purpose | This is why we exist, our compelling purpose. |
| **HOW** | Core Values | These are our two to three core beliefs or principles that define how we do what we do. |
| **WHAT** | Core Definition | This is the straightforward and unambiguous definition of our business focus. |
| **HOW** | Core Strategy | This is the plan for how we see ourselves achieving our goals as a team. |

When we are clear at all four levels, we embody laser clarity, a key aspect of healthy teams.

Group or shared clarity is only half of the story. Healthy teams can clearly articulate their collective answers to these four questions. In addition, they become extremely clear about their unique role and individual contribution to team success.

## UNIQUE (INDIVIDUAL) CLARITY

Teams that are able to align personal strengths with personal areas of responsibility and focus will achieve greater results and experience greater individual and team satisfaction. Working toward *alignment*, getting the right people doing the right things, is a goal worthy of focused effort by each team member for the sake of the whole.

There is a commonly held adage that there is no I in team. I disagree. The no-I thinking suggests that the key to teamwork is to somehow lose individuality for the sake of the team as a whole. This, again, is a type of uniformity that does not reflect a healthy view of diversity.

**The healthy team is made up of many I's who are clear about who they are and the unique strengths that they possess for the sake of the team.**

Personal growth begins with this clarity of knowing our individual strengths and talent patterns.

## INDIVIDUAL STRENGTHS

People should spend most of their time working from their strengths. As it has been said, "If you enjoy what you do, you never work a day in your life." They should not be expending significant energy on a daily basis trying to be something they are not naturally. In my work with clients, I sometimes see a pattern evidenced in a significantly different adapted style versus natural behavioral style.[150] When people are trying to be and do things that don't come naturally, they exert a lot of effort. We usually either adapt for one of two reasons: to succeed or to survive (fear). This is normally experienced as stress. This is always a good place for self-examination regarding the causes of adapting. There are three classic conflicts that drive our perceived need to adapt:

**Table 11.** Three Conflicts That Drive Behavioral Adapting[151]

| Possible Causes for Adapting Behaviorally | |
|---|---|
| **You–Me Conflict** | Adapting my behavioral style to someone around me (a significant individual in my work or personal life) |
| **Me–Job Conflict** | Adapting my behavioral style to my perception of my job requirements or demands |
| **Me–Me Conflict** | Adapting my behavioral style as a way of experimenting with a new version of myself |

Adapting for any of these three reasons drains us. We are, in essence, trying to be someone we are not naturally. Any of us can do this situationally and for a short time. However, when we attempt to be someone else too much of the time, we experience significant stress. It wears us out.

Being who we are requires self-understanding. Individual clarity begins with an accurate and unapologetic embrace of our

---

150 In the TTI Trimetrix EQ™ Report, we show both the respondent's natural behavioral style (who they are at rest or under extreme stress) and their adapted style (how they behave in their current environment). The difference between these two results is the degree of adaptation around each of the four dimensions of DISC. For additional information on behavioral styles, see appendix A.

151 TTI Boot Camp materials.

natural patterns. Individual strengths and talent patterns exist on many different levels. Each behavioral style and combination of all four DISC dimensions in each member of the team suggests strengths that can be capitalized by the team. The same is true with motivators. Especially in these two values-neutral areas, self-acceptance and self-understanding are foundational for individual clarity. Clarity begins with the wisdom of Socrates, "Know thyself." Certain roles on the team are more fitting for members with certain behavioral styles and motivators. Our job is to connect team members' strengths with key team results. This is called alignment.

## ALIGNMENT

Having an accurate view of self that includes a growing understanding of individual and unique talent patterns and expertise is the first step in achieving alignment. The goal is to get the right team members performing the right tasks and having the right focus for maximum team benefit and results. When people work from their strengths, they achieve better results, experience less stress, and maximize team impact. This is a win, win, win.

Often, individuals are assigned roles and duties that are not consistent with their respective behavioral style, motivators, or other significant personal patterns.[152] When this happens, there is misalignment and results and personal satisfaction are hindered. To avoid misalignment, we need to let the position talk to the individual's talent pattern. When we get these two

152 This is commonly the result of an insufficient hiring protocol that fails to utilize job benchmarking and candidate assessment against the benchmark as a key part of the hiring and selection process. Price Associates (TTI) has developed a clear process that greatly improves the likelihood of more accurate hiring, employee retention, and lower turnover that is also compliant with EEOC guidelines.

in alignment, we create great synergy and momentum toward achieving greater results.

## ROLE CLARITY

Role clarity is the personal clarity that a team member has regarding his or her specific role as it relates to team success. It answers the questions, what part do I have to play? and what aspect of team success do I carry? Many employees do not have much clarity when it comes to their role on the team, their personal *why*, *how*, or *what*. It is far too common to see a job description during the hiring process and never to revisit it after being brought onboard.[153] This potential detachment between individuals and their natural strengths and the clear expectations of a given role is too frequently present.

The job description they were shown during the interview process was something they obviously had no participation in or ownership. To obtain greater role clarity, it is important to directly involve those whose roles are being clarified. When people create their own key results or accountabilities, they are far more willing and able to stay focused on obtaining them.

## KEY RESULTS THAT REFLECT SUPERIOR PERFORMANCE

In working with clients to hire new team members (job benchmarking and onboarding) and to increase role clarity for existing team members, I help facilitate the development of key results or accountabilities. Key results answer the question, why does this job exist? Team members describe the results that characterize excellence and superior performance in the position. For

---

153 Onboarding is a specific part of the hiring and selection process as developed by TTI.

sustained focus and usefulness, we normally recommend that each team member have between three and five key accountabilities. The process of creating and utilizing the list is as follows:

1. **Create Key Accountabilities**

   Develop a list of three to five key results. Use subject matter experts for new hires or use team members for those in existing positions. Key results are not merely tasks to be done. They are key or significant results that clearly identify superior performance in a given role by the entire team. Each key result may have subresults that correspond. Make certain that key results are measurable outcomes.

2. **Prioritize Key Accountabilities (Order of Importance)**

   Sort key results by order of importance. Which is most critical for overall success?

3. **Estimate Time for Each Accountability (Out of 80 Percent)**

   Assign a percentage to each key result. This is the percentage of time (out of 80 percent) per week or month that the employee will focus on this result.[154]

4. **Monitor Actual Results on a Timely Basis**

   Far too often, job descriptions are used for hiring, evaluations, and little else. Key results should be referred to on a daily and weekly basis for improved results.

Key accountabilities are different than typical job descriptions. Most job descriptions list off far too many tasks for any one

---

154 It is estimated that every position will have a certain amount (20 percent) of mundane and/or unpredictable distractions from pursuing key results. This inefficiency is almost impossible to eliminate. In light of this reality, the remaining time (80 percent) can be focused on obtaining key accountabilities.

individual to stay focused on daily. The tasks assigned haven't been self-assigned, but rather given or even imposed onto the employee. There is a difference between a task-oriented job description and a clear set of key results.

Individual clarity culminates in the development and fulfillment of key results that are consistent not only with the needs of the team but with the strengths and experience of the individual in each unique role.

**Individual clarity exists in these two key areas: knowing who we are and knowing what our specific role is in regard to results.**

The connection between these two is the degree of alignment according to clarity.

## GETTING CLEAR

When clarity happens at both the group and individual level, a very powerful dynamic is at work. Creating laser focus, in both the narrowing effect and the production of energy, differentiates extraordinary teams from mediocre ones. At the opposite pole from laser clarity is diffused ambiguity. In an ambiguous team environment people are unclear about either the shared big picture of values, goals, and beliefs of the team or their own place at the table. When both are unclear, people tend to lack confidence and hold back from passionately pursuing those things that are valued the most.

Many organizations and teams lack clarity, which contributes to a lack of cohesiveness. These two always feed off of one another. We need to know who we are, what we are about, what our specific part to play consists of, and to live in an environment of deep trust and safety. When these are all present, we begin to experience positive consequences. Before we discuss consequences, there is an all-important team reality that we need to clarify. Communication is the means by which healthy teams have relationships.

# 11

## CLEAR COMMUNICATION

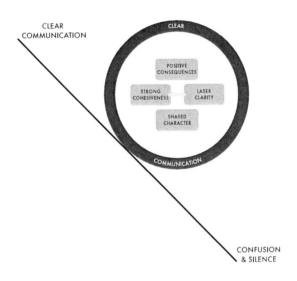

## THE IMPORTANCE OF COMMUNICATION

I remember watching reruns of *The Twilight Zone*. One particular episode stands out in my memory. It was titled, "Where is everybody?" and featured a young Earl Holliman playing a lunar astronaut who had spent the last twenty days in a sensory deprivation chamber as part of his training. In isolation, his mind created a fantasy of being the last man standing on a deserted planet. He was driven to the brink of despair in the midst of his isolation. Like the astronaut in *The Twilight Zone*, we also need to connect with each other. Being connected is part and parcel of the healthy human condition.

Communication has been identified from earliest of times as our greatest need. Human beings are fundamentally communicative. It is this area, however, that often underlies the disintegration of relationships and teams. Despite our focus in corporate America for the last thirty or forty years, most teams still need deeper skill development in this area, which is critical to mission success. One woman recently told me, "One of the biggest stressors in my job now is that the leadership who initially communicated with me often and made me feel valued, almost never communicates with me anymore."

**If we are unable to communicate well, we cannot succeed.**

I love the way Shawn Hayashi reflected this understanding. In her book, *Conversations for Change*, she rightly placed communication as the central, most important aspect to effect change and development in organizations and teams. It is the catalyst that drives systemic change.

For this reason, the Healthy Teams model illustrates communication as the skill that holds the team together and keeps it moving and growing toward greater degrees of health and positive consequences. Communication is spherical. It rolls either downhill or can be pushed uphill with team members working in concert with one another toward deep change. *Communication encircles and defines the team. It is the means of relationship.*

## THE MEANS OF RELATIONSHIP

Knowing someone, having a relationship with them, is dependent upon communication. By definition, a stranger is someone with whom we have never communicated. Being estranged from someone usually indicates that we are not in communication with them. Communication encircles and forms the boundary of healthy teams. Healthy teams build relationships and accomplish shared goals through the use of this primary relational tool.

Too many business models treat communication as a means to an end (typically financial success). Communication then becomes something we need to improve pragmatically to increase our bottom line. "I don't have to like my team members, but I do need to learn to communicate with them, even while holding my nose." This is a utilitarian view of communication. In the Healthy Teams model, communication is both a means and an end. We communicate to accomplish other things as a team, but the communication is valuable in itself as an intrinsic good. Healthy teams value relationships, and communication is simply the expression of this value. We have relationships that provide great joy and satisfaction because of how we communicate with each other.

## STRATEGIC COMMUNICATION PLAN

We enjoy doing things that come naturally. Some things are easier for us to master than others. Some of us, in fact, are more naturally wired for certain kinds of communication than others. We most often attempt to communicate with others in the way that we prefer to be communicated with ourselves. Improving communication is hard work.

Successful organizations and teams adopt a comprehensive and strategic plan for the development, improvement, and maintenance of superior communication. It is not enough to attend a one-day seminar every other year. Sustained focus and attention to the mastery of communication skills are needed. The following is based largely on the teaching of my mentor, Ron Price. This strategic plan has been taught to many organizations and has contributed to their success. Here's the model that Ron taught me (with a few additions and variations):

## SIMPLICITY

The old adage reads: keep it simple stupid. An old proverb reads: where words are many, sin is not absent. Complexity is not necessarily our friend when it comes to communication. Effective communication is first and foremost clear. There is a time and place for complexity. Some subjects, such as conflict, require a more complex approach to rightly understand and unpack meaning that can be derived from a deeper probe. Sometimes, however, we make things overly complex at the expense of clarity. Simplicity in communication calls for us to take the extra step to boil down our message to the important data that the receiver needs to know and understand and to not encumber the message with superfluous words.

## RELEVANCE

When communication is irrelevant, people stop listening. If a company's meetings are filled with unimportant information, attendees will naturally begin to tune out of the conversation. It is of utmost importance that we seek to make all of our communication relevant to team needs and development.

To practice this discipline, healthy teams may need to have separate meeting times to communicate with different members of the team regarding issues that are relevant to them. When communication is thoughtfully kept relevant to all parties in the loop, engagement and participation remain high. We naturally care about those things that we deem are relevant to our role and the team as a whole.

# REPETITION

According to Ron, it takes the average American nine times to fully comprehend and integrate a message. In light of that fact, we need to be comfortable with a reasonable level of repetition in communicating key pieces of information with the team.

Patrick Lencioni has witnessed a repetitive phenomenon among those in leadership roles. He commented that "many leaders fail to overcommunicate because they get bored saying the same things over and over again."[155] Often, leaders make the mistake of assuming that because they have spoken an important concept once or twice, every member of the team is clearly aware of their intention. It is critical that information be repeated as needed to ensure clear team understanding. It is critical that information be repeated as needed to ensure clear team understanding. (You can reread that last sentence seven more times if it helps you get the point.)

# MEDIUMS

Say what needs to be said simply. Make certain that the content of your communication is relevant to the person with whom you are seeking to communicate. Repeat yourself as necessary (check for understanding if unsure). In addition to these three, practice the art of utilizing different and appropriate mediums of communication. People differ in their preferred manner of communication. Some work well with e-mail, others with phone calls. For some, written communication is very helpful. We have the technological possibility of video conferencing. And, saving the best for last, good old face-to-face conversations are our best option.

---

155 Lencioni, *The Advantage*, 143.

Whichever mediums you utilize, always be mindful that body language comprises up to 70 percent of the entirety of communication. You will most certainly want to use several ways to reach a diverse audience. When possible and appropriate, face-to-face uninterrupted meetings are still the preferred option. Table 12 lists various mediums of communication with considerations for each.

**Table 12.** Comparison of Different Mediums of Communication

| Mediums of Communication | Advantages | Disadvantages |
|---|---|---|
| **Face-to-Face** | • Body language<br>• Social intelligence | • Requires physical proximity / availability |
| **Video Conference** | • Some body language (facial expressions)<br>• Limited social intelligence | • No physical connection<br>• Facial expressions but no body language |
| **Phone Conversation** | • Little technology required<br>• Tone of voice | • No physical connection<br>• No body language |
| **Written Communication** | • Careful composition<br>• No potential for interpersonal conflict in the moment | • Lacks emotional context<br>• Can be overthought<br>• Requires interpretation |
| **E-mail**[156] | • Immediate<br>• Easy to send<br>• Free | • Lacks emotional context<br>• Subject to negative interpretation<br>• No feedback loop<br>• Can be overthought<br>• Requires interpretation |

156 As Daniel Goleman wisely pointed out, with e-mail there is a negative bias and no feedback loop, which can lead to impulsive problems like "flaming" where someone sends a furious e-mail as an emotional reaction to an e-mail received and hits "send." See his LinkedIn post, "The danger of email," http://www .linkedin.com /today/post/article/20130222162001-117825785-the-danger-of-email.

| Mediums of Communication | Advantages | Disadvantages |
|---|---|---|
| **Texting** | • Immediate<br>• Easy to send<br>• Free | • Lacks emotional context<br>• Subject to errors<br>• No feedback loop<br>• Overly brief for important discussions<br>• Can be overthought<br>• Requires interpretation |

Whichever medium we choose to utilize, it is important that we clearly and consciously weigh the advantages or disadvantages of each and choose wisely for the benefit of team health.

## STYLES (DISC)

Each of the behavioral styles as measured on the DISC has preferred communication patterns.[157] To be effective, the speaker needs to adapt to the behavioral style of the listener as much as possible. In healthy teams, both sides are aware of behavioral styles and always seek to adapt accordingly. When in doubt as to the listener's style, assume a high S until proven otherwise.[158] Table 13 outlines a few key characteristics of each high style related to communication.[159]

---

157 See appendix A: Behavioral Styles (How)

158 Forty percent of the population is classified as high S on the DISC.

159 Communication guidelines adapted in part from Ron Ernst, *RealTime Coaching Summary* (Carmel, IN: Leadership Horizons, 1999) and from Bonstetter and Suiter, *Universal Language*, 37–98.

**Table 13.** Behavioral Style Communication Characteristics

| Behavioral Style | Body Language | Tone of Voice | Content (Words) |
|---|---|---|---|
| **High D** | • Keeps distance<br>• Strong handshake<br>• Direct eye contact<br>• Leans forward<br>• Hand in pocket | • Strong<br>• Clear<br>• Confident<br>• Direct<br>• Fast pace | • Results<br>• Now, immediate<br>• Bottom line<br>• Challenge<br>• Lead the field<br>• Win |
| **High I** | • Gets close<br>• Smiles<br>• Relaxed, fun<br>• Friendly eye contact<br>• Expressive gestures<br>• Animated | • Enthusiastic<br>• Persuasive<br>• Fast pace<br>• Friendly<br>• High energy<br>• High and low modulation | • Fun (party)<br>• I feel<br>• Socialize<br>• Recognition<br>• Exciting<br>• Picture this<br>• Everyone will be there |
| **High S** | • Relaxed, calm<br>• Methodical<br>• Leans back<br>• Arms crossed<br>• Friendly eye contact<br>• Small gestures | • Warm, soft, calm<br>• Steady<br>• Low tone volume<br>• Slow pace<br>• Careful<br>• Rational<br>• Masked emotions | • Step-by-step<br>• Help me out<br>• Guarantees, promises<br>• Thinks about it<br>• Take your time<br>• Reasonable<br>• Logical |
| **High C** | • Keeps distance<br>• Sits across from<br>• Firm posture<br>• Direct eye contact<br>• Little or no hand gestures | • Controlled<br>• Direct<br>• Thoughtful<br>• Precise<br>• Little modulation<br>• Slow pace | • Here are the facts<br>• The data shows<br>• Proven<br>• Take your time<br>• No risk<br>• Analyzes<br>• Guarantees |

# TIMELINESS

Healthy teams that enjoy good relationships practice the discipline of timeliness as it pertains to communication. Especially for some of the behavioral and communication styles that are prone toward pessimism (high C, low I), a prompt response to an inquiry is extremely helpful and thoughtful. When communication is delayed, often an unintended yet powerful message is conveyed to the one waiting. Inner dialogue (head trash) sometimes kicks in and starts interpreting silence incorrectly and in a way that begins to lessen team cohesion.

Trust is built on trustworthiness. Part of practicing trustworthiness is learning to respond to others in a timely way. This communicates that they are important to us, that we have heard and received their message, and that we don't want to leave them hanging. Healthy teams should discuss and arrive at a general rule of thumb for timely responses inside of the team and with customers and clients.

# CASCADING (MULTILEVEL) MESSAGES

Cascading messages use the proverbial grapevine within the organization. Key messages from the leadership team are communicated with the entire organization through this sequence of cascading levels. This is really a form of social or communication networking within the organization or team.

Leadership teams should come out of their meetings with a clear understanding of what was decided to be communicated with whom, by whom, and by when. They initiate the chain of communication as they provide helpful and necessary information to those who are directly affected by decisions as they are being made. They don't leave room for speculation or misinformation (both of which destroy team cohesion).

## RECIPROCAL (NOT TOP-DOWN)

This is relational communication. Healthy relationships are two-way streets. Both people benefit from the opportunity to communicate, both being heard and understood. Unhealthy teams often suffer from a hierarchal form of communication that leaves those on the receiving end feeling unheard and misunderstood. Messages are simply given as orders or directives with little or no opportunity for discussion or buy-in on the part of the receiver.[160]

Healthy teams communicate in both directions, up and down the organizational chart. This is based in large part on effective listening—listening to understand. There are four levels of listening as shown in Table 14.[161]

**Table 14.** Four Levels of Listening

| Levels of Listening | Problems / Advantages |
|---|---|
| **1. Pretending to Listen** | · Not real listening<br>· May be multitasking while pretending |
| **2. Listening to Fix / Respond** | · Cutting off speaker with suggestions<br>· Failing to hear whole problem<br>· Lacking empathy |
| **3. Listening Autobiographically** | · "That reminds me of a situation in my life . . ."<br>· Listener thinking he or she understands<br>· Some empathy (perhaps better described as sympathy) |

160 High D behavioral styles especially need to make additional effort to practice two-way communication. Their strengths in being directive and decisive can become weaknesses if overused with team members. On the other hand, the high S and C styles need to practice greater assertiveness and provide good feedback to the high D.

161 Ron Price, "Disciplines of Extraordinary Teams" (2004–2013).

| Levels of Listening | Problems / Advantages |
| --- | --- |
| **4. Listening to Understand** | • Focusing on the speaker (content and emotion)<br>• Accurate understanding (content and emotion)<br>• Accurate paraphrasing of content<br>• Accurate reflection of feelings |

Healthy teams practice level 4 listening with one another. Team members feel heard, valued, and important, and cohesion increases dramatically among the team.

## REMOVING DISTRACTIONS (REDUCING INCIVILITY)

We live in a world filled with distractions. Think about the average meeting and the potential for distractions to hinder effective communication. Conference rooms are often prominently placed as focal points off of the main reception area with beautiful glass walls offering an ongoing view of the activities in the lobby. Most of us carry cell phones that alert us to new e-mail, new text messages, incoming calls, and reminders of various sorts.

Because of these distractions, people's attention spans seem to shorten day by day. Some have suggested that this is a result of our media culture of sound and video bytes. Whatever the case, it is imperative for healthy teams focused on communicating well to resist the human distraction of a shortened attention span.

Christine Pearson and Christine Porath studied the impact of incivility on organizational success. Incivility, as they defined it, is "the exchange of seemingly inconsequential inconsiderate words and deeds that violate conventional norms of workplace conduct."[162] Incivility can be understood as a product of reduced character in general or of lowered emotional intelligence in particular. It directly impacts the effectiveness of team communication as it imposes the following distractions:

- Interrupting, talking over colleagues in meetings

- Talking loudly outside and adjacent to meeting rooms

- Arriving late, not respecting the schedule of others who come on time

- Not introducing newcomers or visitors in a meeting

- Checking e-mail or texting during a meeting

- Not saying "please" or "thank you"

- Talking down to or belittling others in meetings

- Inappropriate use of profanity or vulgarity

Many of these acts of incivility become emotional distractions. Team members are triggered through our bad behavior and the result is decreased communication effectiveness. Healthy teams establish clear norms and guidelines and hold one another accountable as a means of maintaining the highest possible opportunity for excellent communication.

## GIVING AND RECEIVING FEEDBACK

Implementing the nine aspects of the strategic communication plan described thus far will produce health and clarity on the

162 Christine Pearson and Christine Porath, *The Cost of Bad Behavior: How Incivility Is Damaging Your Business and What to Do about It* (New York: Penguin Group, 2009), 12.

team. It will bring many levels of benefit, reducing stress levels and internal noise that result from insufficient or ineffective communication. There is one special form of communication that needs to be added to the nine already listed.

### The tenth, capstone communication skill is giving and receiving feedback.

Feedback is a higher order skill that healthier teams learn to master. On both sides of this means of communication, many team members feel ill prepared to practice it well. Giving feedback can be difficult. On one hand, we worry about unintentionally hurting people's feelings. On the other, we worry about sugarcoating our feedback so badly that the message is not conveyed. Receiving feedback isn't easy either. We often struggle to receive even the best-intentioned feedback that in the moment can feel like an assault on our ego.

To help teams develop this capstone communication skill, here are three principles of giving and receiving feedback that will prove extremely useful.[163]

- **Always recognize that there are two experts in every conversation.**

    This first principle is huge. As discussed in chapter 1, we are each unique and different in a myriad of ways. These differences shape our perspectives on conversations and relationships. These two different viewpoints are always in play as we seek to give and receive feedback. Here are the two expert positions:

    - *I* am the expert of my *intent*.
    - *You* are the expert of my *impact*.

---

163 Price, "Disciplines."

- **Always give feedback for the benefit of others.**

  Be aware of hidden agendas. Make sure that the feedback you are giving to team members is truly in *their* best interest and intended to help *them* improve. Here are a few questions to ask yourself before you speak:

  - Is it true and accurate (not just my opinion)?
  - Is it necessary?
  - Is it helpful (will they benefit from receiving my feedback)?

- **Always receive feedback as a true professional.**

  Receiving feedback is a learned and valuable skill. Most of us have room for improvement in this area. Here are some helpful guidelines to help personal growth:

  - Is the feedback true or does it contain partial truth?
  - Is it helpful in some way (can you apply it and grow from it)?
  - Practice suspending judgment (emotional regulation). Gather feedback data as objectively as you can (process it later). Try not to defend yourself initially in the moment.
  - Practice good listening skills (write comments down if you need to, paraphrase, check for understanding, etc.)
  - Practice saying "thank you."

## WORTH OUR EFFORT

If there is one area that teams will see immediate benefits from, it is this area of improved communication. The insight from teams that incorporate behavioral style, motivator, and emotional intelligence assessment information into their daily interaction is substantial. Often, it is like a light coming on. Team members begin to see clearly the dynamics that are occurring within them, within others, and between them as they interact.

The strategic communication skills can all be learned and practiced. If we are serious about working toward positive consequences, we can move the corporate culture of communication toward health in these ways. Communication is the means of relationship.

## TO REVIEW, HERE ARE THE TEN PARTS OF A STRATEGIC COMMUNICATION PLAN:

1. **Keep it simple.**
2. **Keep it relevant.**
3. **Repeat yourself as necessary.**
4. **Use different mediums as appropriate.**
5. **Adapt to others' DISC styles.**
6. **Practice timely responsiveness.**
7. **Use cascading messages.**
8. **Have reciprocal (two-way) conversations (include level 4 listening).**
9. **Remove distractions (including incivility).**
10. **Give and receive feedback for team health.**

# 12

## POSITIVE CONSEQUENCES

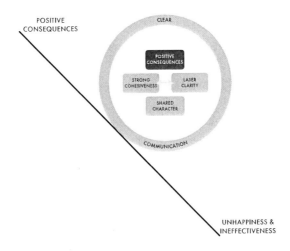

## THE LAW OF NATURAL CONSEQUENCES

Consequences are the end results of our choices. Though there are other confounding variables complicating this simple equation, in the end we, for the most part, reap what we have sown. To clarify, there is such a thing as misfortune or tragedy and, on the opposite hand, even dumb luck that contributes to our success at times. It is a misconception, however, that organizational health just happens. Doing nothing will almost certainly guarantee that it won't happen. Entropy is real. Trying harder doesn't guarantee that it will. But without our ongoing focused effort and intentionality, the outcome is predictable.

We began this journey together by noticing the many levels and sorts of differences between us. Some of those make it more difficult for us to find success, but they never preclude it. The field isn't level, but it is playable as long as we have breath. Every living human being has an opportunity to rise to the challenge called life and to overcome, to find the good life, happiness, or whatever else we want to call ultimate meaning. No level of adversity renders the situation hopeless. There are many examples of the resiliency of the human condition to remind us of the possibilities we each possess.

This is not to somehow invalidate the pain that so many feel as a result of the mistreatment of others and the misfortune of life. Our sufferings are real. We ought to care about the stories of others around us that remind us of the imperfections of this life. Deep empathy, entering into the pain of others, is a crucial part of mature humanity. So, we care deeply about the pain of the past and encourage those who have fallen or been tripped to get up and return to the race in due time. We love a comeback and root for underdogs.

**Consequences, the natural and related outflow of decisions and choices, are built into the world around us.**

Consequences can provide helpful feedback. They give us an opportunity to reconsider our current plan of action. If what I'm doing is producing the wrong set of consequences, I have the option of changing the plan. In either case, whether positive or negative consequences, a message is being conveyed to those who have ears to hear it or eyes to see it. Consequences of either sort are inevitable. How then do we create a higher potential for the experience of positive consequences? What are the positive consequences we are looking for as a team anyway?

# POSITIVE CONSEQUENCES

As a result of the active pursuit of team health through the exercise of shared character, strong cohesion, laser clarity, and in an environment characterized by clear communication, we greatly increase our odds for experiencing the following positive consequences of fully participating on a healthy team:

## INTRINSIC ENJOYMENT

The first gain is the most obvious and the most often overlooked—increased "inherent satisfaction with the activity itself."[164] We have been steeped for so long in the idea that the means lead to an end that we don't know how to find joy, delight, and meaning in the means themselves. Doing good work is a reward in itself.

As we embrace this worldview, we begin to achieve a more autotelic personality. As Mihaly Csikszentmihalyi pointed out,

> 'Autotelic' is a word composed of two Greek roots: *auto* (self) and *telos* (goal). An autotelic activity is one we do for its own sake because to experience it is the main goal.[165]

There is no deeper answer to why we do what we do than the enjoyment we derive from doing it. As a culture we are beginning to remember this source of joy and meaning we have forgotten.

---

164 Pink, *Drive*, 75.

165 Csikszentmihalyi, *Finding Flow*, 117.

254          PUSHING BACK ENTROPY

## INCREASED ENGAGEMENT, CREATIVITY, AND FLOW

As we work and live in an environment of secure attachment (strong cohesion), shared clarity around common purposes and values (culture), undergirded by strong character and in clear relationships with those around us, we begin to experience increased engagement. As noted, a significant disparity between aspirational and practiced values creates disengagement. The inverse is also true, as we align what we say we're about with what we actually practice, we begin to see a marked increase in engagement.

With elevated engagement and feelings of safety and belonging, creativity increases. Where fear, groupthink, and uncertainty are removed and replaced with trust, respect, and confidence, our ability to think outside the box is enhanced. We begin to enter into more frequent, though unplanned, experiences of flow.

> What is common to such moments is that consciousness is full of experiences, and these experiences are in harmony with each other. Contrary to what happens all too often in everyday life, in moments such as these what we feel, what we wish, and what we think are all in harmony. These exceptional moments are what I have called *flow experiences*. The metaphor of "flow" is one that many people have used to describe the sense of effortless action they feel in moments that stand out as the best in their lives. Athletes refer to it as "being in the zone," religious mystics as being in "ecstasy," artists and musicians as aesthetic rapture.[166]

When we experience flow, we experience the most harmonious aspect of life that yields the most extraordinary results. The experience of more frequent flow is a reward in itself.

---

166 Csikszentmihalyi, *Finding Flow*, 29 (italics added).

## EXISTENTIAL GAINS

In these healthy environments, team members begin to realize experiential gains that directly impact their existence as human beings. They begin to live in increased freedom from the constraints, demands, and stresses of the typical work environment. They experience increases in meaning and significance as they wholeheartedly face the challenges life throws at them.

Healthy teams experience the positive consequence of rising above the futility and meaninglessness that so often characterizes the workplace, the stuff on which *Dilbert* or *Dunder-Mifflin* is based. Teams that conspire together to create holistic cultures reap the reward of a more fully human existence.

## ACCOMPLISHMENT OF CORE MISSION

Teams focused on core values and purpose tend to more fully realize both. The core purpose for any organization or team needs to be a lofty and ideal goal. As the team moves toward health, it moves ever closer toward the purpose for which it exists. The dream for which the team strives begins to be more realized before their eyes. This, again, is the reward itself.

## IMPROVED HEALTH

We have used the term health mainly in the sense of being functional, the opposite of dysfunctional. Here, it means quite literally health: physical, mental, or emotional. As the team moves toward health, the members' individual health improves, including stress levels, heart rate, blood pressure, and immune system. Just as importantly, they experience greater emotional health in the form of less depression, anxiety, or other symptoms of mental distress. The positive consequences of pursuing team functionality are quite tangible and can be measured in the bodies and minds of team members.

## DEEPER, MORE SATISFYING RELATIONSHIPS

All of the effort toward team health results in improved relationships. Relationships are enjoyed for what they are, a reward in themselves. They are not viewed as a means to another end. They are not utilitarian relationships. As a result of the intense focus on personal and interpersonal health, team members typically experience an overflow of gain in other relationships outside the team. Marriages are strengthened. Relationships with children improve. The entire relational world of those fortunate enough to be counted part of these healthy teams improves exponentially.

## AND MORE MONEY

More money in itself doesn't make people happier. There is a threshold of having enough materially. Beyond that, having more is only a very small factor in overall self-rating of personal happiness. Daniel Pink described this reality that flows directly from our increased understanding of motivation 3.0:

> Type I [*intrinsic motivation-based*] behavior does not disdain money or recognition. Both Type X [*extrinsic motivation-based individual*]'s and Type I's care about money. If an employee's compensation doesn't hit the baseline [*enough*]—if her organization doesn't pay her an adequate amount, or if her pay isn't equitable compared to others doing similar work—that person's motivation will crater, regardless of whether she leans toward X or toward I. However, *once compensation meets that level, money plays a different role for Type I's than Type X's*. Type I's don't turn down raises or refuse to cash paychecks. But one reason fair and adequate pay is so essential is that it takes people's focus off money, which allows them to concentrate on the work itself. By contrast, for many Type X's, money is the table. It's why they do what they do.[167]

---

167 Pink, *Drive*, 77 (italics added).

The work is the end itself. The money, beyond meeting the needs of the employee for fair compensation and providing a living, becomes far less of a motivator and does not produce the happiness promised. Csikszentmihalyi examined the data related to the relationship between material well-being and happiness. He first noticed that the data indicates that people who live in wealthier nations have a higher self-rating of happiness.

> But within the same society there is only a very weak relationship between finances and satisfaction with life; billionaires in America are only infinitesimally happier than those with average incomes. . . . beyond the threshold of poverty, additional resources do not appreciably improve the chances of being happy.[168]

Having made the point that money itself and more of it doesn't necessarily make us happier, does an increase in team health lead to a healthier bottom line? Lencioni helps us think about the answer to this question:

> The financial cost of having an unhealthy organization is undeniable: wasted resources and time, decreased productivity, increased employee turnover, and customer attrition. The money an organization loses as a result of these problems, and the money it has to spend to recover from them, is *staggering*. . . . Turning an unhealthy company into a healthy one will not only create a massive competitive advantage and *improved bottom line*, it will also make a real difference in the lives of people who work there.[169]

There are no losers, except those companies that refuse to recognize the signs of their own ill health and avoid treatment that could lead them toward renewed vitality.

**Organizational health is a win–win proposition.**

---

168 Csikszentmihalyi, *Finding Flow*, 20.

169 Lencioni, *The Advantage*, 13 (italics added).

# RECOGNITION, REWARDS, AND MOTIVATION 3.0

The American workplace has historically operated according to an assumption about human motivation that Daniel Pink referred to as motivation 2.0. In his book, *Drive: The Surprising Truth about What Motivates Us*, Pink defined motivation 2.0 by two principles: *"Rewarding an activity will get you more of it. Punishing an activity will get you less of it."*[170] This carrot-and-stick approach to motivation, though outdated and outmoded as Pink went on to demonstrate, is still the prevalent thinking in much of the American workplace today. Pink explained how in the latter half of the twentieth century things moved a little bit toward motivation 2.1—the same fundamental assumption but with a relaxed dress code and a more flexible schedule. We still thought extrinsic motivation was the way to get results.

Pink's research-based observations demonstrated the fallacy in this theory of extrinsic motivation. What Pink discovered is that extrinsic motivation only works in a very small bandwidth of functions—repetitive more menial tasks, things that are becoming less a part of the American workplace with the advent of technology. For creative tasks, Pink found extrinsic motivation is a hindrance. What we need is an upgrade to motivation 3.0, to discover the importance of intrinsic motivation as a means of moving employees to higher levels of achievement and group and individual satisfaction.

Positive consequences are far broader and more comprehensive than merely financial rewards. They are all-inclusive. They include financial aspects but go far beyond a motivation 2.0 or 2.1 world to see the whole-life benefits that result from the

---

170 Pink, *Drive*, 32 (italics added).

fulfillment of intrinsic motivation. Healthy teams achieve and create success at all levels.

## IMPLEMENTATION IS THE KEY

Whether by slow incremental change, pushing uphill, or through the cataclysmic, crisis-driven deep change that Quinn advocated, moving away from slow death is hard work. It would be easier to do nothing. That decision, however, will result in the team moving by default toward the entropy of slow death.

If the robust positive consequences of an ongoing pursuit of team health are real, the question then becomes, how do we get there? Talking about the principles in this book or in a myriad of other books on leadership and team development is one thing. Actually applying these principles in the midst of a real team—our team—is another. Consequences flow from our decisions and commitments or lack thereof. Teams determined to pursue health undertake the following measures to assure implementation.

## SYSTEMS, STRUCTURES, AND PROCESSES

In order to achieve positive consequences, teams that are willing to commit to the pursuit of health establish appropriate systems, structures, and processes that amplify and enable team success. Systems, as we have noted, are powerful. That power can be leveraged for good or it can be allowed to be destructive.

Healthy teams challenge and change the existing system, particularly its structures and processes that dampen team success. One of the greatest enemies to positive change is the status quo. Great teams talk about and alter the culture over time. They aren't afraid to address the sacred cows that have developed, and they work together to eliminate unhelpful broken systems to replace them with new alternatives to move the group toward health.

Structure itself is not the enemy, but often overstructure or unnecessary structure can be. Bellman and Ryan wisely reminded us that great teams

> never forget that the main reason they are together is about fulfilling their purpose. The structure is a means to that end. . . . More organic than mechanical, members work together in ways that are collaborative, flexible, creative, and adaptive. They create just-enough structure—at the time that it is needed—to support purpose and outcomes.[171]

The objective is to find the just-right balance between overstructure and understructure for the team. Sometimes structure is inserted as a substitute for clarity. With ever-increasing individual and group clarity, the need for overstructure is lessened.

Healthy groups of all kinds have processes that assist in self-monitoring and maintaining organizational clarity and direction. Processes are a means of mutually agreeing how to work through or approach an objective together. They are always descriptive of interpersonal dynamics and relationships. When we have a clear process, we have a clear path toward continuous improvement on all fronts.

## PERFORMANCE EVALUATION

Unfortunately, the words "performance evaluation" have come to mean a formal employee review complete with the fear and awkwardness of sitting down with one or more supervisors whom we may or may not have a close relationship with and reviewing numeric and written feedback about our performance

---

171 Bellman and Ryan, *Extraordinary Groups*, 24.

over the last year. This formal process generally does not produce great results in either improved performance or the trans-
mission of helpful feedback or evaluation.

**Healthy teams establish a method of *ongoing*
performance evaluation.**

They don't wait for a formal sit-down once a year. They build into
the culture regular and repeated times where they ask themselves, how are we doing? Evaluation, helpful feedback, and
continuous improvement are all a part of the constant healthy
conversation among the team.

Healthy teams clearly understand their core purpose, their
values, their business definition, their big picture strategy for
success, their individual roles and how those fit together in the
team, and the key results that the team looks to each member
to provide. These are the standards, the metrics, against which
the team is able to evaluate its progress. The team develops the
habit of constantly evaluating itself against these benchmarks.
This is much healthier and much more effective than the stereo-
typical evaluation we have all regrettably experienced.

## CONTINUOUS IMPROVEMENT

Each of us is unique. We approach this area of ongoing performance evaluation and continuous improvement differently.
The key is to understand how we can best provide the structures, systems, and processes that will serve us well. This is not
a case of one-size-fits-all. Cookie-cutter approaches most often
fail. The team commitment to continuous improvement and
increased health must be reflected in a consistent and helpful
manner of measuring progress over time. The specifics of the
plan that best serve the team are left for the healthy capable

team to configure. The main concern is to invest the time and energy into crafting a plan for success.

## CONSEQUENCES BEGET CONSEQUENCES

Results are often seen as ends, and we typically utilize the means to achieve them. The Healthy Teams model advocated is more organic than that. In this model, team health is pursued as a goal and as the means toward goal fulfillment. The system gives continual feedback to the team as it moves forward over time.

The team experiences a never-ending cascade of feedback loops.[172] Greater health in terms of positive consequences filters back into and through the system and begets greater health. We never arrive but begin to enjoy the journey toward more complete humanity in a way we haven't before. Life begins to be lived more fully. We move away from the slow death of organizational and corporate life toward a whole new experience.

---

172 According to research in the field of emotional intelligence, we are looking for at least a 5:1 ratio of positivity to negativity on the team. John Gottman, in his research with married couples, suggested a minimum ratio of 4:1 as a predictor of marriages enduring.

# CONCLUSION

# DEFYING ENTROPY

To do nothing is to do something. To the extent that we do not work against it, the principle of organizational entropy will continue to lead us away from healthy team development, key results, and the achievement of shared goals. Teams that don't practice won't win. Ignoring conflict prevention will increase the likelihood of experiencing significant team dissension and division. A lack of focus on the development of team health will result in the inevitable consequence of ill health. Yes, this sounds like and is a lot of work. This work, however, doesn't need to be burdensome.

**Entropy moves us slowly toward death. The principles contained in this book invite us to life.**

Life lived to the fullest is our invitation and opportunity. We as teams can decide to reject the status quo, resist the problem of entropy, defy the odds, and become the best version of ourselves and our team possible. We can defy this principle of entropy every day as we choose to fight in the opposite direction. The ball can be moved uphill. Health is attainable and rewards us with itself as we push through to our shared goal.

All that has been said in this volume will accomplish nothing if we do not understand it, internalize it, and apply it. Entropy is a powerful force and a mighty foe. It is not easily overcome. It mocks those who make feeble or inconsistent attempts to defeat it. It has remained from the beginning of time as teams have shipwrecked against its rocky shore. Your team can be the exception to the rule. You can work together to fight this principle of decay. To beat it, it will require all of you giving all you've got, laying aside your baggage and choosing to move boldly and vulnerably forward as a team.

*Alone we can do so little; together we can do so much.*

## — Helen Keller

You are invited to take the assessment of team health on the following pages. Compare your thoughts with others on your team and begin to discuss areas of focus for your team to move forward.

# TEAM HEALTH CHECKLIST

*(check all that apply)*

## CHARACTER

☐ I consistently connect my aspirational values with my practiced values.

☐ As an organization, we consistently live according to our published and professed values.

☐ Our current tribal stage is closest to (circle one):

1            2            3            4            5

## EMOTIONAL INTELLIGENCE

☐ I am growing in self-awareness. I know what I am feeling and why.

☐ I exercise emotional regulation and am growing in my ability to bring myself back to a calm, unemotionally hijacked state.

☐ I don't give up when confronted with adversity. I keep going in spite of obstacles.

☐ I understand how others are feeling and am able to empathize with them (put myself in their shoes).

☐ I have good social skills that allow me to build great working relationships with my teammates.

☐ We are cocreating a culture of ever-increasing emotional intelligence.

## ETHICS

☐ I abide by ethical standards that govern my profession.

☐ I adhere to organizational policies and live according to our agreed-upon norms of conduct.

☐ I live honestly before my teammates. I make it a practice not to lie or to shade the truth (fudge, embellish, use half-truths, etc.)

☐ I work hard at having personal integrity and authenticity.

☐ I make myself personally accountable to my teammates for my attitudes and actions.

☐ I exercise impartiality in my judgments and decisions, putting the best interest of the team ahead of my self-interest.

☐ I am growing in humility and am aware of my areas of weakness and failure.

☐ I exercise moral courage; I do the right thing even when it costs me personally.

☐ I have courage to be vulnerable with my teammates.

☐ I am loyal to my teammates, do not talk behind their backs, and defend them when others criticize them.

☐ I seek to be trustworthy, to live in such a way that I can be trusted by my teammates.

☐ We are cocreating a culture of high ethical aspirations.

## COHESION

☐ I feel bonded to my teammates at a fairly deep level.

☐ Our culture is one of trust rather than fear.

☐ We are connected to each other because we enjoy one another.

☐ We hold each other mutually accountable.

☐ Trust is something we value highly and always seek to deepen.

☐ We see vulnerability as a strength, not a weakness. It is inspirational.

- ☐ We engage in rigorous debate. We don't have groupthink or fear in our team meetings and discussions.
- ☐ We fully participate in the process of forming our team and pursuing results together.
- ☐ We each own the decisions of the team as a whole and do not undermine our joint decisions.

## CLARITY

- ☐ We continue to invest significant time and effort to remain clear on our common purpose and values.
- ☐ We continue to seek greater alignment between our key results and our individual talent patterns.

## GROUP CLARITY

- ☐ I am extremely clear on why we exist (our core purpose).
- ☐ We are extremely clear on why we exist (our core purpose).
  - We exist to

    _____

    _____

- ☐ Our core purpose informs everything we do (it's not just a plaque on the wall).
- ☐ I am extremely clear on our core values.
  - Our core values are

    _____

    _____

- ☐ We are extremely clear on our core business definition.
  - Our business definition is

    _____

    _____

☐  We are extremely clear on our current core strategy.

- Our core strategy is

_____

_____

## INDIVIDUAL CLARITY

☐  I am extremely clear on my

- place in the organization (team).
- personal talent patterns critical for our health/ success.
- personal areas of potential weakness.
- role (key responsibilities that reflect superior performance).

## COMMUNICATION

☐  We adapt our communication with others based on our understanding of their DISC styles.

☐  We use cascading messages frequently to convey critical information.

☐  We strive to keep meetings relevant to everyone in attendance.

☐  We use different mediums to communicate with different people on the team as appropriate to their preferences.

☐  We respond to each other in a timely manner.

☐  We practice active (level 4) listening with each other.

☐  We are good at giving and receiving feedback.

☐  I am growing in my ability to give helpful feedback.

☐  I am growing in my ability to receive feedback from others.

## CONSEQUENCES

☐  I love working here and being part of this team.

☐  I have a great sense of satisfaction that comes from accomplishing the things we do together.

☐  I love working with my coworkers.

☐  Some of my closest relationships are with those I work with.

☐  We have high levels of engagement on the team.

☐  We are making significant strides toward achieving our core mission and purpose.

☐  We have low stress levels on the team.

☐  There is little fear among team members.

☐  We are profitable and doing well financially, both as a team and individually.

☐  We challenge broken systems and seek to change them.

☐  We constantly evaluate ourselves and our performance (in healthy ways and in light of our key results).

☐  We strive for continuous improvement as a team.

☐  We regularly celebrate wins as a team together.

☐  My teammates help me become a better person.

☐  My relationships at work and outside of work are improving.

# EPILOGUE

# I HAVE A DREAM

*Prophets* and *philosophers* tend to be perfectionists, and *the imperfections of life offend them.* Whereas the rest of humankind is glad to be alive, imperfections and all.[173]

Prophets speak to the moral condition of the society and call the people back to renewal and restoration. Philosophers help us think deeply about our worldview and definition of the good life. Both get a bad rap. Historically, prophets are told to shut up and sit down. People often don't want to hear about the ways in which they are dysfunctional. Philosophers are similarly seen as real downers, party killers. They think way too much for our taste, and if they are discouraged or despairing, it's their own fault for trying too hard to understand life.

The glaring imperfections of dysfunctional organizations and teams ignite a passion in me to want to do what I can to help things move toward renewed health, vitality, and holistic results. For me, conflict is painful and something that can and should be eliminated from the majority of our day-to-day experiences. I can see a picture of healthy teams emerging from the chaos and entropy, teams willing to move toward a new paradigm.

---

173 Csikszentmihalyi, *Finding Flow*, 19 (italics added).

I have a dream . . .

> *of a world with less conflict, where people learn to value each other, where we resist the urge to get what we feel entitled to when it comes at someone else's expense, where people when they do hurt each other, admit it, repair the damage, and try with all that is in them to truly restore relationships. It's not a world where we fake it and pretend it doesn't exist or it didn't happen, but a world where we look evil, injustice, and oppression in the eye, even when it's our reflection in the mirror, and refuse to let it win.*

> *of a world with healthy relationships of trust and vulnerability, where team members achieve unimaginable results as a by-product of becoming fully human, where the best qualities of humanity are on display consistently in all spheres of our lives, where there are less disconnects, less compartmentalization, less incongruity, where we find joy and meaning intrinsically in what we do and how we do it, where character once again undergirds our understanding of the good life.*

We can't get to this possible world by avoiding the conversation. So, because I am passionate about seeking to bring this world into existence, I invite you to a conversation you've been avoiding. Conflicted about conflict? Most of us are. Nonetheless, accept the invitation to discuss something you may find troubling or confusing. As you begin to prevent conflict, you are well on the way to developing team health. I invite you to continue your journey as a team toward health by seeking to fully implement the suggestions in this book that will lead your team toward these ideals.

I wish you all the best as you embark on your journey together,

Andy Johnson

*Nampa, Idaho, 2013*

# APPENDIX A

# BEHAVIORAL STYLES (HOW)

## OBSERVABLE PATTERNS OF BEHAVIOR: HOW WE INTERACT WITH OTHERS

People are different. We all have predictable and recognizable tendencies—idiosyncrasies. At the level of observable behavior, these are seen and experienced by those around us. We each have certain recurring patterns of behavior that answer the question of *how* we behave. The DISC[174] has four primary behavioral dimensions. They each deal with slightly different aspects of our overall behavioral style.

- The **D dimension** relates to how an individual deals with *problems and challenges.*

- The **I dimension** relates to how an individual uses influence with *people and contacts.*

- The **S dimension** relates to how an individual deals with *pace and change (consistency).*

---

174 There are various versions of the DISC assessment in use today. DISC is based on the original work of William Marston, the author of *Emotions of Normal People.* Price Associates is a value-added associate of Target Training International (TTI), a leading DISC assessment company that has developed the R4 version, factoring in all four responses to each item.

- The **C dimension** relates to how an individual relates to *procedures and compliance (constraints)*.

## EIGHT PRIMARY STYLES, EACH IS UNIQUE

Many versions of the DISC assessment yield results that fall into one of four dominant categories (high D, high I, high S, high C). Dominant traits may or may not be found on the high side of the graph, however. Approximately 30 percent of the population possesses a dominant trait on the low side (low D, low I, low S, low C). The dominant behavioral trait for any individual is that trait(s) furthest from the 50 percent midpoint (the energy line). This means that there are actually eight primary behavioral styles:

- **High D style.** Dominant traits of this style include *decisive, driving, determined, competitive, bold, pioneering, short-tempered, strong-willed, aggressive.*

- **Low D style.** Dominant traits of this style include *indecisive, unsure, hesitant, low-keyed, undemanding, cautious, mild, agreeable, modest, peaceful.*

- **High I style.** Dominant traits of this style include *optimistic, persuasive, charismatic, inspiring, convincing, trusting, friendly, magnetic.*

- **Low I style.** Dominant traits of this style include *pessimistic, distrusting, critical, moody, logical, undemonstrative, skeptical, suspicious, matter-of-fact.*

- **High S style.** Dominant traits of this style include *accommodating, systematic, logical, patient, relaxed, unhurried, long-tempered, steady, loyal, team-oriented, poker-faced.*

- **Low S style.** Dominant traits of this style include *emotional, expressive, impetuous, impulsive, flexible, impatient, restless, active, demonstrative.*

- **High C style.** Dominant traits of this style include *precise, perfectionistic, orderly, diplomatic, accurate, meticulous, detailed.*

- **Low C style.** Dominant traits of this style include *creative, nonconforming, individualistic, free-spirited, fearless, careless, independent, unsystematic, uninhibited.*

Each individual's style is a composite of all four behavioral dimensions, not only defined by the dominant trait(s).

## THE SHADOW SIDE OF EACH STYLE

An important aspect of the theory behind the DISC assessment is that it is values-neutral. There is no right or wrong style, no better or worse, only different along four dimensions. This is very important for teams to understand. It is fairly common for team members to assume that their dominant trait is the "right" style and to suggest, either subtly or more explicitly, that others on the team should be more like them.[175] The existence of this attitude suggests a fundamental misunderstanding of the DISC theory.

While each style and fourfold score is values-neutral, there is a potential for weakness with each of the strengths. The way we normally express this possibility is to say that *an overused strength becomes a weakness.* Here are just a few examples of this potential problem:

- The overused optimism (strong positive bias) of a high I can become misrepresentation of the truth (spin).

- The overused stability and wisdom of a high S can become stubbornness and resistance (digging in).

---

175 Often it is the high D style that thinks this way.

Each of the four high styles has a corresponding shadow side that can be seen. Consider the following shadows for each of the four styles below:

**Table 15.** Potential Shadows of High Behavioral Styles

| High Style | Potential Shadow |
|---|---|
| **High D** | • Runs over others<br>• Uses people as things<br>• Angry outbursts<br>• Aggression or bullying |
| **High I** | • Misrepresents the truth<br>• Manipulative<br>• No follow-through<br>• Too many dreams and ideas not thought through |
| **High S** | • Stubbornness, rigidity, resistance<br>• Resentment<br>• Lack of assertiveness<br>• Passive–aggressive |
| **High C** | • Judgmental, self-righteous, critical of others<br>• Overly self-critical<br>• Fearful<br>• Paralysis by analysis |

These shadow sides often come out in the midst of emerging conflict. Knowing our potential downfall as it relates to our individual DISC profile can be very useful information to help us work to prevent conflict as a team.

## BEHAVIORAL STYLES AND CONFLICT

Each of us has a unique blend of the four dimensions of behavioral patterns. In general, we tend to get along more readily with those who are like us. However, effective teams are most often comprised of a variety of behavioral styles interacting harmoniously together. So for the sake of the team, we learn how to adapt to styles that differ from our own. Each of the four high styles has a predictable response to conflict.

**Table 16.** Behavioral Styles and Conflict

| Behavioral Style | Typical Approach to Conflict | Implications |
|---|---|---|
| **High D** | Enjoy (Win) | • Can initiate and sustain conflict as sport<br>• Can be aggressive, intimidating in conflict<br>• Short memory of conflict<br>• Recovers quickly |
| **High I** | Run Away | • Biggest fear of social rejection kicks in<br>• Conflict seen as negative (avoidance)<br>• Prefers positive experiences<br>• Uses humor to avoid, diffuse situation |
| **High S** | Tolerate (Store Up) | • Puts up with a lot<br>• Often struggles with resentment from previous conflicts<br>• Defensive when backed into corner (high D)<br>• Sometimes takes offense for others (loyalty) |
| **High C** | Avoidance | • Looking for facts / proof in conflict (objective)<br>• Highly sensitive to perceived criticism<br>• Confront carefully w/ facts |

Some styles are more difficult to blend with one another. Conflict, at a behavioral level, can predictably be found in the following combinations:

# THE "RULES" CONFLICT: LOW C VERSUS HIGH C

Low C individuals tend to be indifferent or negative toward rules, policies, or procedures. As Randy Lisk recently described it, "High Cs are rule keepers, low Cs are rule breakers, and extremely low Cs are rule makers." When this low C runs into a high C, conflict frequently occurs. The low C is perceived as a rule breaker by the high C. The high C seems too uptight and bound up with rule keeping to the low C. This is the fuel for the impending conflict. All it takes to set it off is a demand that is blocked.

# THE "PACE" CONFLICT:
# HIGH D VERSUS LOW D (HIGH S OR C)

High D individuals are "can do, get it done" people. We need them to lead us, particularly in times of crisis. Because they do not get bogged down in overanalysis, they allow us to move quickly as a team. On the other end of the spectrum are high C or S people (low D). They are good at comprehensive and thoughtful analysis. They are assets to the team, helping us find problems in our ill-conceived plans and strategies. They tend to slow things down. The radical difference in pace often contributes to the development of conflict on the team.

# THE "ATTITUDE" CONFLICT:
# HIGH I VERSUS HIGH C (LOW I)

High I people tend to be optimistic. They see life through positive lenses and often retell past events through this filter of positivity. High C or low I individuals tend toward pessimism. One sees the glass half full, the other half empty. They have a built-in potential to irritate each other. This is one of the most volatile combinations on the team.

# THE "TRUTH" CONFLICT: HIGH C VERSUS HIGH I

The optimism of high I individuals tends to flavor the way they recall and retell past events. For the detailed and fact-based orientation of the high C individual, this can often feel like the high I person is not being truthful. Conflict emerges from this perception of dishonesty on the part of the embellishing I. Again, C and I are the most volatile mix of styles.

## HEALTHY TEAM BUILDING AND BEHAVIORAL STYLES

Healthy teams fully leverage the different behavioral styles of the team. They practice the belief that behavioral styles are values-neutral and do not value one style over another. They recognize that it takes the level of behavioral diversity they have as a team to succeed.

**Healthy teams work to understand their own styles and the styles of the others on the team, so they can better communicate and work with others.**

They incorporate the language of DISC into their daily interactional life, and it informs everything they do. DISC gives teams a new vocabulary with which to discuss team dynamics and interaction. It shapes tribal culture in a permanent way.

## SUMMARY

Behaviors are the language of *how* we do what we do. Understanding our behavioral style and the different styles of others on the team allows us a much greater opportunity to adapt toward them for greater communication, cohesiveness, and results. It is important for each of us to learn the whole language of DISC, not just the aspects related to our strengths. Knowing the styles of those around us and seeking to understand and value their different way of behaving are essential to the development of healthy teams.

# APPENDIX B

# CORE MOTIVATORS (WHY)

## WHAT DRIVES US?

Why do we do what we do? The answer to this question is found in our personal values, our passions, our motivators. We all tend to pursue those things we find most valuable and to be indifferent or negative toward those things we don't value. Motivators explain the underlying force behind the why of what we do. We consistently act according to our personal values.

**We pursue things we are most passionate about, and we are indifferent or hostile toward things we do not value.**

This explains the way in which we condemn and judge one another. We roll our eyes and scoff about those things we do not value that others do. We consider those things that others are passionate about as illegitimate or "stupid" pursuits. Motivators underlie conflict at a deeper level than behavioral styles.

## WHAT ARE MOTIVATORS?

Eduard Spranger (1882–1963), a German psychologist and philosopher, identified six primary motivators that explained reasons why we do what we do, our extrinsic motivation, that we find among human beings:[176]

- **Theoretical.** The drive to understand, to know and to understand. This drive often combines with other drives so that we seek to understand in order to fulfill another drive.

- **Utilitarian.** The drive to see results, to realize return on investment (ROI) in financial or other aspects.

- **Aesthetic.** The drive to experience beauty and harmony in the environment and in relationships.

- **Social.** The drive to help and serve others.

- **Individualistic.** The drive to have power, leadership, and influence.

- **Traditional.** The drive to live by a set of principles and to help others live similarly.

In the Motivator section of the TTI reports used with clients, each motivator is expressed as a score between 12 and 72. The population mean is also indicated for each of the six motivators. This is important information. If we are significantly below the population mean in a certain motivator, it means that we are far less passionate or indifferent or even negative about that drive than most people around us. If we are significantly above the mean, it means that we may be viewed by others as being overpassionate or even overbearing as we seek to live out our passion.

---

176 Bill Bonstetter, the CEO of TTI, significantly updated and improved the theory and assessment of motivators.

## MOTIVATORS AND CONFLICT

Behavioral styles and personal motivators are not correlated. In other words, any behavioral style can have any motivator underlying it. We cannot see motivators like we can behaviors. This means that we must learn about the motivation of others through conversation, observation of their passions, or the use of assessments.

Motivators are near to the core of the individual and dictate the *why*. Why (motivators) is a deeper dimension than how (behaviors). Conflict can be exacerbated at the level of behavioral styles. It is even more likely that differences around values will propel the potential for interpersonal conflict. The motivator aspect of a conflict is readily observed when comparing two conflicting individuals' motivator bar graphs side by side. Here's what normally becomes apparent:

## YOUR TOP TWO VERSUS MY BOTTOM TWO

Our top two motivators drive us. Our middle two are situational. We tend to be indifferent or negative toward our bottom two. Conflict is intensified by the presence of significantly different motivator profiles. We often use these specific differences to attempt to devalue our opponent in the midst of the battle. Here's an example to help explain:

Sally's top motivator is social. That means her primary drive is to help others. Her lowest motivator is utilitarian. She would say that she's not about money and has a hard time with people who care too much about material things. Bill, her boss, has a top motivator of utilitarian. He has used this drive to create a very successful insurance business, from which Sally has benefitted by working there for twelve years. Bill's bottom motivator is social.

**Our inner dialogue about others and "what's wrong with them" often centers around motivators.**

It is usually some version of "what they care about is stupid as opposed to what really matters (what I care about)." We use this devaluation as a means of condemning our opponent for not caring about the right things. The inner dialogue of Bill and Sally might look something like this:

Bill (thinking about Sally):

- She's a bleeding heart.

- If I let her, she'd give everything we own away to the poor and we'd be out of business.

Sally (thinking about Bill):

- He only cares about money. He's a money-grubber.

- He doesn't care about people, just the bottom line.

Notice these are thoughts, not openly expressed statements. We rarely say things of this nature to one another, but we do think them. Our inner attitude toward others finds expression in various ways. These inner attitudes that Bill and Sally have could quite easily add fuel to their growing conflict that erupts as they attempt to work together to plan the company Christmas party.

# ORGANIZATIONAL VALUES AND PERSONAL VALUES MISMATCH

Organizations, tribes, or teams have cultures. Those cultures tend to be built on the shared values of leaders that influence the values of the company. When individuals have personal values (motivators) that differ significantly from the corporate values of the organization or group, they will often experience feelings of disconnection and conflict with other team members. This results in being the "odd person out."

Whereas behavioral differences are normally able to be viewed and utilized as a means to greater team results, there are occasions where a significant value or motivator difference can prove to be catastrophic to continued team harmony. Sometimes an individual's personal passions are not in alignment with the corporate culture. This is simply a mismatch. There are no right or wrong things to value, but there are situations when the differences are detrimental to continuing to work together toward common ends.

## MOTIVATORS AND HEALTHY TEAM BUILDING

Knowing how our passions differ from others on the team is the beginning of understanding one another. Most often, devaluation and judgment occur in the context of motivators. We deem that the things that really matter, that drive our teammates' behavior, are unimportant. We are indifferent or negative toward their core passions. Healthy teams don't interact like this. They know and understand the different drivers of the members of the team and respectfully seek to utilize the diverse passions to achieve the core purpose of the team.

## SUMMARY

Motivators describe those things that drive us, that fuel our passion, that help others understand why we do what we do. Healthy teams understand others' differing personal values and motivators and resist the urge to judge drives that are opposite to their own.

# APPENDIX C

# EMOTIONAL INTELLIGENCE (EQ)

## WE ARE EMOTIONAL CREATURES

The Stoics in ancient Greece succeeded in large part in leaving us a heritage in the West that devalues the emotional life. The highest good for a person of character in ancient Greece was often identified as *apatheia* (apathy). Being apathetic or indifferent, unaffected by the vicissitudes of life, was seen as the height of human development. This ideal may sound noble on the surface, but it inherently contradicts something we all deal with every day—feelings.

**We are emotional creatures, deeply so.**

Beginning in the mid-1990s, the relevance of this fact began to be made exceedingly clear. With the rapid advances in technology, brain science in the last few decades has increased exponentially. We understand far more than ever the importance of emotionality to the overall well-being and healthy development of human beings.

## WHAT IS EMOTIONAL INTELLIGENCE?

We are becoming quite clear about the importance of a trait called emotional intelligence (EQ). Daniel Goleman defined emotional intelligence as including

> abilities such as being able to motivate oneself and persist in the face of frustrations; to control impulse and delay gratification; to regulate one's moods and keep distress from swamping the ability to think; to empathize and to hope.[177]

Cooper and Sawaf defined emotional intelligence as

> the ability to sense, understand, and effectively apply the power and acumen of emotions as a source of human energy, information, connection, and influence.[178]

Yale psychologist, Peter Salovey, described the five domains of emotional intelligence. Goleman summarized his findings as follows:

1.  *Knowing one's emotions.* Self-awareness—recognizing a feeling as it happens—is the keystone of emotional intelligence.

2.  *Managing emotions.* Handling feelings so they are appropriate is an ability that builds on self-awareness.

3.  *Motivating oneself.* Marshaling emotions in the service of a goal is essential for paying attention, for self-motivation and mastery, and for creativity.

4.  *Recognizing emotions in others.* Empathy, another ability that builds on emotional self-awareness, is the fundamental "people skill."

5.  *Handling relationships.* The art of relationships is, in large part, skill in managing emotions in others.[179]

---

177 Goleman, *Emotional Intelligence*, 34.

178 Robert Cooper and Ayman Sawaf, *Executive EQ: Emotional Intelligence in Leadership and Organizations* (New York: Berkley Publishing Group, 1996), xiii.

179 Goleman, *Emotional Intelligence*, 43.

Building on this fivefold model, Izzy Justice and Target Training International (TTI) developed an assessment that measures the presence of emotional intelligence in these five domains.

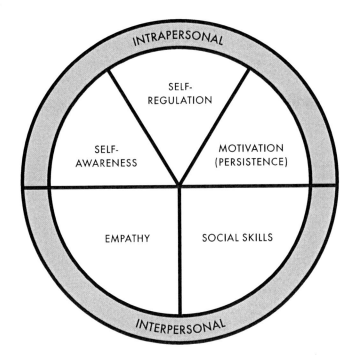

**Figure 15.** The five aspects of emotional intelligence.

These five hierarchal traits are understood in two separate and interrelated halves: intrapersonal and interpersonal. The foundation of emotional intelligence is found in intrapersonal development.

## INTRAPERSONAL EQ

Emotional intelligence begins within each of us internally or intrapersonally. Intrapersonal EQ consists of three interrelated traits that build on one another in the following order. Let's begin with the skill of self-awareness.

## Self-Awareness

Self-awareness is the ability to correctly identify one's current affective (emotional) state and to understand the context in which it is occurring. This is the ability to name, with ever-increasing specificity and accuracy, what is being felt at any given moment and why. Emotions are experienced bodily. With increased self-awareness, one is highly attuned to bodily signals of an emotional state.

## Self-Regulation

Knowing what we're feeling and why is one thing. We need to learn to regulate or control the downward emotional spiral. It takes approximately four hours for any of us to recover from an emotional hijacking, an emotionally laden incident that triggers deep feelings within us. The skill of self-regulation allows us to bring ourselves back to a calm state in a shorter period of time. This always reminds me of the famous tennis player John McEnroe. He was a great player but is most famous for his emotion.

## Motivation

People with low EQ will often give up in the midst of high emotion as a result of adversity or obstacles. Instead of marshaling strength to get through difficulties, they too quickly throw in the towel. We can easily observe this behavior in small children. Motivation is a trait that grows with our overall maturity as adults. We have a myriad of examples of this intrapersonal trait of EQ in the heroes who have fought against cancer and won. Their courage to persevere and to fight is what is called motivation in our model.

# INTERPERSONAL EQ

In addition to understanding ourselves intrapersonally, people with higher levels of EQ are able to understand the emotions of others. We move from knowledge of self to knowledge of others with the critical skill of empathy.

## Empathy

Empathy is the ability to rightly understand what others are feeling, their current emotional state and temperature. When we read their emotional state rightly, we are able to interact in a healthy way with others around us. This again is a learned skill that is a key component of interpersonal EQ and relationships. This is one of the traits that is most notably lacking in individuals who tend toward narcissism and entitlement.

## Social Skills

This is the culminating skill. Putting all of these skills together, the person with high social skills is able to successfully manage relationships (including the critical emotional aspect) to develop deeper cohesion, good communication, and greater team results. This includes the critical skill of emotional attunement, the ability to connect successfully with others and to track with them at a deep level.

# EMOTIONAL INTELLIGENCE AND CONFLICT

Emotional intelligence serves as a general and foundational prevention against escalation into conflict. Team members who are emotionally healthy and mature are much more aware of their own internal emotional states, as well as the states of their teammates. They have learned how to regulate their emotions, which pays off huge dividends in the midst of potentially heated disagreements. They don't simply fly off the handle at others because they are having a bad day. They can talk intelligently with others about what they are feeling and why and find support.

Teams with characteristically low EQ create dangerous environments. Emotional negativity is toxic to the workplace and spreads like cancer throughout the team. In fact, team leaders with low EQ can bring down the level of the entire team and lead to bullying. Bullying or workplace mistreatment of others is normally practiced by those who embody a toxic mix (low self-awareness, low self-regulation, low empathy).

Emotional intelligence is one-half of character. Teams that strive together for shared character in the form of increased emotional intelligence are indirectly but effectively working to prevent conflict.

## EMOTIONAL INTELLIGENCE AND TEAM BUILDING

We have emphasized numerous aspects of healthy teams in this volume. None is perhaps as mission-critical as the development of emotional intelligence by each member of the team. The results that flow from increased emotional intelligence are amazing. It is one of the secrets of healthy teams. As job complexity increases, so do the possible rewards of increases in emotional intelligence. Consider the following findings:[180]

- Clerks, machine operators—3x more productive with high EQ

---

180 Justice, *EQmentor*, as derived from Cary Cherniss, "The Business Case for Emotional Intelligence" (1999), accessed November 9, 2013 at www.eiconsortium .org/reports/business_case_for_ei.html. See also John Hunter, Frank Schmidt & Michael Judiesch, "Individual Differences in Output Variability as a Function of Job Complexity," *Journal of Applied Psychology*, 75, no. 1 (February 1990), 28–42.

- Sales clerks, mechanics—12x more productive with high EQ

- Doctors, consultants—127x more productive with high EQ

Jobs in today's workplace are tending more and more toward the complex and away from the mundane. With the advent of technology, things that can be done by machines are leaving the jobs that require the best in human beings who are capable of complex problem solving and have high levels of creativity.

## SUMMARY

Emotional intelligence matters. It has the ability to make or break an individual or a team. Increases in emotional intelligence contribute exponentially to individual and team health. Organizations that are serious about moving away from slow death know that emotional intelligence is a primary means of moving uphill.

# APPENDIX D

## THE EMPEROR'S NEW CLOTHES

Many years ago there lived an emperor who loved beautiful new clothes so much that he spent all his money on being finely dressed. His only interest was in going to the theater or in riding about in his carriage where he could show off his new clothes. He had a different costume for every hour of the day. Indeed, where it was said of other kings that they were at court, it could only be said of him that he was in his dressing room!

One day two swindlers came to the emperor's city. They said that they were weavers, claiming that they knew how to make the finest cloth imaginable. Not only were the colors and the patterns extraordinarily beautiful, but in addition, this material had the amazing property that it was to be invisible to anyone who was incompetent or stupid.

"It would be wonderful to have clothes made from that cloth," thought the emperor. "Then I would know which of my men are unfit for their positions, and I'd also be able to tell clever people from stupid ones." So he immediately gave the two swindlers a great sum of money to weave their cloth for him.

They set up their looms and pretended to go to work, although there was nothing at all on the looms. They asked for the finest silk and the purest gold, all of which they hid away, continuing to work on the empty looms, often late into the night.

"I would really like to know how they are coming with the cloth!" thought the emperor, but he was a bit uneasy when he recalled that anyone who was unfit for his position or stupid would not be able to see the material. Of course, he himself had nothing to fear, but still he decided to send someone else to see how the work was progressing.

"I'll send my honest old minister to the weavers," thought the emperor. He's the best one to see how the material is coming. He is very sensible, and no one is more worthy of his position than he.

So the good old minister went into the hall where the two swindlers sat working at their empty looms. "Goodness!" thought the old minister, opening his eyes wide. "I cannot see a thing!" But he did not say so.

The two swindlers invited him to step closer, asking him if it wasn't a beautiful design and if the colors weren't magnificent. They pointed to the empty loom, and the poor old minister opened his eyes wider and wider. He still could see nothing, for nothing was there. "Gracious," he thought. "Is it possible that I am stupid? I have never thought so. Am I unfit for my position? No one must know this. No, it will never do for me to say that I was unable to see the material."

"You aren't saying anything!" said one of the weavers.

"Oh, it is magnificent! The very best!" said the old minister, peering through his glasses. "This pattern and these colors! Yes, I'll tell the emperor that I am very satisfied with it!"

"That makes us happy!" said the two weavers, and they called the colors and the unusual pattern by name. The old minister listened closely so that he would be able say the same things when he reported back to the emperor, and that is exactly what he did.

The swindlers now asked for more money, more silk, and more gold, all of which they hid away. Then they continued to weave away as before on the empty looms.

The emperor sent other officials as well to observe the weavers' progress. They too were startled when they saw nothing, and they too reported back to him how wonderful the material was, advising him to have it made into clothes that he could wear in a grand procession. The entire city was alive in praise of the cloth. "Magnifique! Nysseligt! Excellent!" they said, in all languages. The emperor awarded the swindlers with medals of honor, bestowing on each of them the title Lord Weaver.

The swindlers stayed up the entire night before the procession was to take place, burning more than sixteen candles. Everyone could see that they were in a great rush to finish the emperor's new clothes. They pretended to take the material from the looms. They cut in the air with large scissors. They sewed with needles but without any thread. Finally they announced, "Behold! The clothes are finished!"

The emperor came to them with his most distinguished cavaliers. The two swindlers raised their arms as though they were holding something and said, "Just look at these trousers! Here is the jacket! This is the cloak!" and so forth. "They are as light as spider webs! You might think that you didn't have a thing on, but that is the good thing about them."

"Yes," said the cavaliers, but they couldn't see a thing, for nothing was there.

"Would his imperial majesty, if it please his grace, kindly remove his clothes." said the swindlers. "Then we will fit you with the new ones, here in front of the large mirror."

The emperor took off all his clothes, and the swindlers pretended to dress him, piece by piece, with the new ones that were to be fitted. They took hold of his waist and pretended to tie something about him. It was the train. Then the emperor turned and looked into the mirror.

"Goodness, they suit you well! What a wonderful fit!" they all said. "What a pattern! What colors! Such luxurious clothes!"

"The canopy to be carried above your majesty awaits outside," said the grand master of ceremonies.

"Yes, I am ready!" said the emperor. "Don't they fit well?" He turned once again toward the mirror, because it had to appear as though he were admiring himself in all his glory.

The chamberlains who were to carry the train held their hands just above the floor as if they were picking up the train. As they walked they pretended to hold the train high, for they could not let anyone notice that they could see nothing.

The emperor walked beneath the beautiful canopy in the procession, and all the people in the street and in their windows said, "Goodness, the emperor's new clothes are incomparable!

What a beautiful train on his jacket. What a perfect fit!" No one wanted it to be noticed that he could see nothing, for then it would be said that he was unfit for his position or that he was stupid. None of the emperor's clothes had ever before received such praise.

"But **he doesn't have anything on!**" said a small child.

"Good Lord, let us hear the voice of an innocent child!" said the father and whispered to another what the child had said.

"A small child said that he doesn't have anything on!"

Finally everyone was saying, "He doesn't have anything on!"

The emperor shuddered, for he knew that they were right, but he thought, "The procession must go on!" He carried himself even more proudly, and the chamberlains walked along behind carrying the train that wasn't there.[181]

---

181 Hans Christian Andersen, *Keiserens nye kloeder* (1837), trans. D. L. Ashliman (1999). Andersen's source was a Spanish story recorded by Don Juan Manuel (1282–1348). Accessed October 21, 2013 http://www.pitt.edu/~dash/type1620 .html#andersen.

# INDEX

# ABOUT THE AUTHOR

Andy Johnson's passion in life is to help leaders at all levels feel validated. As leaders embrace their unique talent patterns and stop making excuses for how they naturally are, they lead more consistently from their strengths. As an introvert who thinks deeply and analytically, Andy is convinced that people who are wired similarly need to leverage these abilities for the good of the team around them. He writes extensively on the themes of conflict, introversion, and leadership. One of his greatest strengths is the ability to call attention to the elephants in the room, to ask the questions that teams may be avoiding. At times, he acts like a corporate counselor or a team therapist disrupting team status quo, moving the system to new and healthier places.

Andy is a Team Dynamics Specialist and an Executive Coach of Quiet Leaders (ambiverts and introverts) at Price Associates, an elite team of leadership performance consultants. As he focuses on helping leaders and teams move away from conflict toward greater degrees of health and improved results, he brings his prior experiences as an architect, a business owner, and a therapist to his current work. As an executive coach, he uniquely blends directness and honesty with compassion and understanding. The result is clarity for individuals and their teams, leading to a greater quality of life and improved performance.

Andy is a Certified Professional Behaviors Analyst (CPBA), a Certified Professional Motivators Analyst (CPMA) and a Certified Professional Emotional Intelligence Analyst (CPEQA) with Target Training International (TTI). He holds a Bachelor of Architecture degree from Cal Poly, San Luis Obispo, and a Master of Science in Community Counseling degree from Northwest Nazarene University, Nampa, Idaho. He is a licensed professional counselor in the state of Idaho.

On a personal note, Andy has been part of a marital team for over twenty-five years. He and his wife, Sherri, have learned to share leadership in their family. They have enjoyed the way their natural talent patterns complement each other creating greater synergy. They have been blessed with three grown daughters and one son-in-law and look forward to the joy of grandchildren to help fill the void of their empty nest. Andy is an avid reader and enjoys using his synthesizing ability to bring together concepts of current thought leaders. His deep thinking and attention to detail come through in his writing. Andy and Sherri currently reside in southwest Idaho, having moved from their native California twenty-one years ago. For more information about Andy and his work, see www.price-associates.com and his personal blog at www.introvertrevolution.com.